Modern Critical Interpretations

James Joyce's
A Portrait of the Artist
as a Young Man

Modern Critical Interpretations

These and other titles in preparation

Modern Critical Interpretations

James Joyce's

A Portrait of the Artist as a Young Man

Edited and with an introduction by

Harold Bloom
Sterling Professor of the Humanities
Yale University

Chelsea House Publishers ◊ *1988*

NEW YORK ◊ NEW HAVEN ◊ PHILADELPHIA

©1988 by Chelsea House Publishers, a division
of Chelsea House Educational Communications, Inc.

Introduction © 1988 by Harold Bloom

Printed and bound in the United States of America

10 9 8 7 6 5 4 3 2 1

∞ The paper used in this publication meets the minimum
requirements of the American National Standard for
Permanence of Paper for Printed Library Materials, Z39.48–1984

Library of Congress Cataloging-in-Publication Data
James Joyce's A portrait of the artist as a young man.
  (Modern critical interpretations)
  Bibliography: p.
  Includes index.
  1. Joyce, James, 1882–1941. Portrait of the artist
as a young man.   I. Bloom, Harold.   II. Series.
PR6019.09P6455   1988   823'.912   87-25630
ISBN 1-55546-020-8 (alk. paper)

Contents

Editor's Note

This book brings together a representative selection of the best critical interpretations of *A Portrait of the Artist as a Young Man,* James Joyce's autobiographical novel. The critical essays are reprinted here in the chronological order of their original publication. I am grateful to David Parker and Paul Barickman for their assistance in editing this volume.

My introduction takes sides with William Empson against Hugh Kenner on the issue of how Joyce represented Stephen, whether as a serious and sympathetic young artist, or as a humorless young aesthete. Kenner himself appropriately begins the chronological sequence of criticism with his polemical insistence that the *Portrait* is "a meticulous pastiche of immaturity."

The late Richard Ellmann, Joyce's definitive biographer, shows how in the *Portrait* "the theme of broken friendships represents his hero's broken ties with Ireland and the world." Anthony Burgess, novelist and Joycean, sees the *Portrait* as an advance over *Dubliners* and *Stephen Hero,* because it replaces "a bunch of epiphanies" with a "genetic pattern of symbolic imagery," a pattern of escape from the bondage of the grosser elements in life.

Answering Ellmann, in a sense, Suzette Henke offers a feminist version of Kenner's ironic view of Stephen's character, since she sees Stephen's misogyny and his supposedly egocentric aestheticism as obstacles to artistic maturation. Martin Price, rather more sympathetic to Stephen, judges his aesthetic theory as an attempt to liberate art from social and religious bondage.

Stephen is interpreted as the teller of his own story by John Paul Riquelme, who argues that "a *Portrait* is both the author's autobiographical fiction and the autobiography of the fictional character." Patrick Parrinder, in a superb overview, traces the heritage of Joyce's novel in Wordsworth, Pater, Ibsen, and Wilde, and also illuminates the thematic images of voice and memory in the *Portrait*. This volume concludes with Michael Seidel's study of Joyce's transition from Stephen's Dumas-like version of Romantic renunciation and exile to Leopold Bloom's classical version of Odyssean exile.

Introduction

The late Sir William Empson, in an essay on "Joyce's Intentions," sought to rescue *Ulysses* and *A Portrait of the Artist as a Young Man* from the school of Christianizing critics, called for short by Empson "the Kenner Smear." Though the Kenner Smear essentially baptizes Joyce's writings (following the lead of T. S. Eliot, who found Joyce eminently orthodox), it also deprecates the representation of Stephen, particularly in the *Portrait,* as Empson protested:

> One or two minor points need fitting in here. It is part of Kenner's argument, to prove that Stephen is already damned, that he is made to expound the wrong aesthetic philosophy. Joyce was letting him get the theory right in *Stephen Hero,* but when he rewrote and concentrated the material as the *Portrait* Stephen was turned into a sentimental neo-Platonist; that is, he considered the artist superior to earthly details, instead of letting the artist deduce realism from Aquinas. If we actually did find this alteration, I agree that the argument would carry some weight, though the evidence would need to be very strong. But, so far as I can see, there is only one definite bit of evidence offered, that Joyce in rewriting left out the technical term 'epiphany', invented by himself to describe the moment of insight which sums up a whole situation. I can tell you why he left it out; because he was not always too egotistical to write well. Even he, during revision, could observe that it was tiresome to have Stephen spouting to his young friends about this invented term. But I find no change in doctrine; he still firmly rejects "Idealism, the supreme quality of beauty being a light from some

other world, the idea of which the matter was but the shadow," and explains that the 'claritas' of Aquinas comes when the image "is apprehended luminously by the mind which has been arrested by its wholeness and fascinated by its harmony." This is surely the doctrine which Kenner approves, and we next have as clear a pointer from the novelist as he ever allows us: "Stephen paused and, though his companion did not speak, felt that his words had called up around them a thought enchanted silence." A critic who can believe that Joyce wrote this whole passage in order to jeer at it has, I submit, himself taken some fatal turning, or slipped unawares over the edge of some vast drop.

I am happy to agree with Empson against Hugh Kenner on this, but I myself find Aquinas a surrogate here for Joyce's ghostly aesthetic father, Walter Pater, actual inventor of *Stephen Hero*'s "epiphanies" and so of a mode of intellectual vision that dominates the *Portrait,* remains crucial in *Ulysses,* but largely subsides in *Finnegans Wake.*

Pater founded his criticism upon perception and sensation, the perception of privileged moments of vision, and the sensation of the intensity and brevity of those epiphanies, sudden manifestations or shinings forth of power, order, beauty or of a transcendental or sublime experience fading into the continuum of the commonplace. Like Joyce after him, Pater asked very little of these epiphanies, far less than Wordsworth or Ruskin had asked, let alone the eminently orthodox, from Gerard Manley Hopkins (Pater's student at Oxford) through T. S. Eliot and his New Critical followers, against whom Empson fought his anticlerical campaigns. The essential formula for Stephen's epiphanies in the *Portrait* is set forth in Pater's study of the Renaissance:

> A sudden light transfigures a trivial thing, a weathervane, a windmill, a winnowing flail, the dust in the barn door; a moment—and the thing has vanished, because it was pure effect; but it leaves a relish behind it, a longing that the accident may happen again.

Himself an Epicurean and so a metaphysical materialist, Pater's achievement was to remove from the epiphany its theological and idealistic colorings. Joyce, certainly not a Catholic believer, accepts the epiphany from Pater as a secular and naturalistic phenomenon, purged of its Wordsworthian and Ruskinian moralizings. The Joycean epiphany is still "a sudden spiritual manifestation" in which an object's "whatness" or "soul" can be seen as leaping "to us from the vestment of its appearance." But that is spiritual only in the Epicurean sense, in which the "what" is unknowable anyway, and Joyce is no more Christian than Whitman is in *Song of Myself* when the child asks him what the grass is, or than Stevens is in his apprehension of sudden radiances.

Just before the close of the *Portrait,* Stephen records a vision that is an epitome of epiphanies in a passage both Ovidian and Paterian:

> The spell of arms and voices: the white arms of roads, their promise of close embraces and the black arms of tall ships that stand against the moon, their tale of distant nations. They are held out to say: We are alone. Come. And the voices say with them: We are your kinsmen. And the air is thick with their company as they call to me, their kinsman, making ready to go, shaking the wings of their exultant and terrible youth.

The flight of Icarus and his fall are assimilated to the Paterian sense of belatedness, of coming at the end of a long and high tradition of Romantic vision. Joyce, like Pater, longs for a renaissance, for a rebirth into the company of exiles to worldliness who found another country in the strongest imaginative literature. Ovid, who knew the bitterness of exile, prefigured Dante in at least that regard, and there is a Dantesque quality to Stephen's epiphany here. That hovering company of visionaries is pervaded with the auras of solitude and of departure, and their exultant youth may yield to the terrible fate of Icarus. If this epiphany's eroticism is palpable and plangent, its darker reverberations intimate deathliness as the price of the freedom of art. Echoes of Ibsen and Blake combine in Stephen's famous penultimate declaration:

> Welcome, O life! I go to encounter for the millionth time the reality of experience and to forge in the smithy of my soul the uncreated conscience of my race.

"Forge" is a blacksmith's term in this context, and not a penman's. The very name of Ibsen's *Brand* suggests the heat that can forge what Ibsen's protagonist calls "the uncreated soul of man," and we can remember also Blake's Los at the smithy, hammering out the engraved plates of his vision. Again one votes for Empson, against Kenner, as to the high seriousness of Stephen's aspirations and the aesthetic dignity with which Joyce chose to invest them.

The *Portrait* in Perspective

Hugh Kenner

> From wrong to wrong the exasperated spirit
> Proceeds, unless restored by that refining fire
> Where you must move in measure, like a dancer.
> T. S. ELIOT

> Faites votre destin, âmes désordonnées,
> Et fuyez l'infini que vous portez en vous!
> BAUDELAIRE

> And yet he felt that, however he might revile and mock her
> image, his anger was also a form of homage.
> Portrait

A Portrait of the Artist as a Young Man, which in its definitive form initiates the second cycle, was some ten years in the writing. A 1,000-page first draft was written around 1904–6, about the same time as the bulk of *Dubliners.* This was scrapped and a more compressed version undertaken in 1908; the third and final text was being composed in 1911, and was finished early in 1914. About one-third of the first draft (the *Stephen Hero* fragment) survives to show us what was going on during the gestation of this book, the only one which it cost Joyce far more trouble to focus than to execute.

Joyce first conceived the story of Stephen Dedalus in a picaresque mode. The original title was meant to incorporate the ballad of Turpin Hero, a reference to which still survives in the final text. Turpin spends most of the ballad achieving gestes at the expense of a gallery of middle-class dummies, beginning with a lawyer:

From *Dublin's Joyce.* © 1956 by Hugh Kenner. Indiana University Press, 1956.

> As they rode down by the powder mill,
> Turpin commands him to stand still;
> Said he, your cape I must cut off,
> For my mare she wants her saddle cloth.
>> O rare Turpin Hero,
>> O rare Turpin O.
>
> This caus'd the lawyer much to fret,
> To think he was so fairly bit;
> And Turpin robb'd him of his store,
> Because he knew he'd lie for more.
>> O rare Turpin Hero,
>> O rare Turpin O.

The lawyer's mistake was to admit the plausible stranger to his intimacy. Stephen in the same way achieves a series of dialectical triumphs over priests, parents, and schoolfellows. The typical dialogue commences amid courtesies:

> Stephen raised his cap and said "Good evening, sir." The President answered with the smile which a pretty girl gives when she receives some compliment which puzzles her—a "winning" smile:
> —What can I do for you? he asked in a rich deep calculated voice.

But cut-and-thrust soon follows:

> —May I ask you if you have read much of [Ibsen's] writing? asked Stephen.
> —Well, no . . . I must say . . .
> —May I ask you if you have read even a single line?
> —Well, no . . . I must admit.

Stephen always relieves the interlocutor of his complacence:

> —I should not care for anyone to identify the ideas in your essay with the teaching in our college. We receive this college in trust. . . .
> —If I were to publish tomorrow a very revolutionary pamphlet on the means of avoiding potato-blight would you consider yourself responsible for my theory?
> —No, no, of course not . . . but then this is not a school of agriculture.

—Neither is it a school of dramaturgy, answered
Stephen.

(Stephen Hero)

The ballad ends with Turpin in jail condemned to the gallows; *Stephen
Hero* was presumably to end, as the *Portrait* does, with Stephen Pro-
tomartyr on the brink of continental exile, acknowledged enemy of
the Dublin people. This Stephen is an engaging fellow with an ex-
plosive laugh, an image of the young Joyce whom Yeats compared to
William Morris "for the joyous vitality one felt in him," or of the
student Joyce who emerges from his brother's *Memoir*:

> Uncompromising in all that concerned his artistic integ-
> rity, Joyce was, for the rest, of a sociable and amiable
> disposition. Around his tall, agile figure there hovered a
> certain air of youthful grace and, despite the squalors of his
> home, a sense of happiness, as of one who feels within
> himself a joyous courage, a resolute confidence in life and
> in his own powers. . . . Joyce's laugh was characteristic
> . . . of that pure hilarity which does not contort the
> mouth.

When Stephen's uncompromising side occasionally becomes
absurd, Joyce the recorder is always at hand to supply a distancing
phrase: "the fiery-hearted revolutionary"; "this heaven-ascending
essayist"; "he was foolish enough to regret having yielded to the
impulse for sympathy from a friend." Toward the end of the existing
fragment we find more and more of these excusing clauses: "No
young man can contemplate the fact of death with extreme satisfaction and no young man, specialised by fate or her stepsister chance
for an organ of sensitiveness and intellectiveness, can contemplate
the network of falsities and trivialities which make up the funeral of
a dead burgher without extreme disgust." This clumsy sentence, its
tone slithering between detachment, irony, and anger, is typical of
the bad writing which recurs in the *Stephen Hero* fragment to signal
Joyce's periodic uncertainty of Stephen's convincingness.

The book ran down unfinished in 1906, stalled partly by its own
inner contradictions, partly by the far maturer achievement of
Dubliners. It had never, Joyce saw, had a theme; it was neither a
novel, nor an autobiography, nor a spiritual or social meditation. It

contained three sorts of materials that would not fuse: documentation from the past, transcribed from the Dublin notebooks; Joyce's memories of his earlier self, transmuted by a mythopoeic process only partly controlled; and his present complex attitude to what he thought that self to have been.

Fortunately, the catalytic theme was not long in coming. In the late fall of 1906, he wrote from Rome to his brother about a new story for *Dubliners,* "Ulysses." On February 6, 1907, he admitted that it "never got any forrarder than the title." It coalesced, instead, with the autobiographical theme, and both subjects were returned to the smithy. A novel, *Ulysses,* as Joyce told a Zurich student ten years later, began to be planned as sequel to a rewritten *Portrait.* In 1908 *Stephen Hero* was discarded for good, and the job of lining up the two works began. And once the final balance of motifs for the *Portrait* had been at last struck and the writing of the definitive text completed, the last exorcism, *Exiles,* took only three spring months. *Ulysses* and *Finnegans Wake* took seven and seventeen years, but their recalcitrance was technical merely. The *Portrait* includes their scenario: first "the earth that had borne him" and "the vast indifferent dome" (Penelope, Ithaca), then sleep and a plunge into "some new world, fantastic, dim, uncertain as under sea, traversed by cloudy shapes and beings." These are lyric anticipations of the dense epic and dramatic works to come; the actual writing of those works went forward during the next quarter-century with scarcely a false step.

Linking Themes

In the reconceived *Portrait* Joyce abandoned the original intention of writing the account of his own escape from Đublin. One cannot escape one's Dublin. He recast Stephen Dedalus as a figure who could not even detach himself from Dublin because he had formed himself on a denial of Dublin's values. He is the egocentric rebel become an ultimate. There is no question whatever of his regeneration. "Stephen no longer interests me to the same extent [as Bloom]," said Joyce to Frank Budgen one day. "He has a shape that can't be changed." His shape is that of aesthete. The Stephen of the first chapter of *Ulysses* who "walks wearily," constantly "leans" on everything in sight, invariably sits down before he has gone three paces, speaks "gloomily," "quietly," "with bitterness," and "coldly," and "suffers" his handkerchief to be pulled from his pocket by the exuberant Mulligan, is precisely

the priggish, humourless Stephen of the last chapter of the *Portrait* who
cannot remember what day of the week it is, sentimentalizes like
Charles Lamb over the "human pages" of a second-hand Latin book,
conducts the inhumanly pedantic dialogue with Cranly on mother-
love, writes Frenchified verses in bed in an erotic swoon, and is
epiphanized at full length, like Shem the Penman beneath the bedclothes, shrinking from the "common noises" of daylight:

> Shrinking from that life he turned towards the wall,
> making a cowl [!] of the blanket and staring at the great
> overblown scarlet flowers of the tattered wall-paper. He
> tried to warm his perishing joy in their scarlet glow,
> imaging a roseway from where he lay upwards to heaven
> all strewn with scarlet flowers. Weary! Weary! He too was
> weary of ardent ways.
>
> *(Portrait)*

This new primrose path is a private Jacob's ladder let down to his bed
now that he is too weary to do anything but go to heaven.

To make epic and drama emerge naturally from the intrinsic
stresses and distortions of the lyric material meant completely new
lyric techniques for a constation exact beyond irony. The *Portrait*
concentrates on stating themes, arranging apparently transparent
words into configurations of the utmost symbolic density. Here is
the director proposing that Stephen enter the priesthood:

> The director stood in the embrasure of the window, his
> back to the light, leaning an elbow on the brown cross-
> blind, and, as he spoke and smiled, slowly dangling and
> looping the cord of the other blind, Stephen stood before
> him, following for a moment with his eyes the waning of
> the long summer daylight above the roofs or the slow deft
> movements of the priestly fingers. The priest's face was in
> total shadow, but the waning daylight from behind him
> touched the deeply grooved temples and the curves of the
> skull.

The looped cord, the shadow, the skull, none of these is accidental.
The "waning daylight," twice emphasized, conveys that denial of
nature which the priest's office represented for Stephen; "his back to
the light" co-operates toward a similar effect. So "crossblind":

"blind to the cross"; "blinded by the cross." "The curves of the skull" introduces another death-image; the "deathbone" from Lévy-Bruhl's Australia, pointed by Shaun in *Finnegans Wake,* is the dramatic version of an identical symbol. But the central image, the epiphany of the interview, is contained in the movement of the priest's fingers: "slowly dangling and looping the cord of the other blind." That is to say, coolly proffering a noose. This is the lyric mode of *Ulysses*'s epical hangman, "The lord of things as they are whom the most Roman of Catholics call *dio boia,* hangman god" (*Ulysses*).

The Contrapuntal Opening

According to the practice inaugurated by Joyce when he rewrote "The Sisters" in 1906, the *Portrait,* like the two books to follow, opens amid elaborate counterpoint. The first two pages, terminating in a row of asterisks, enact the entire action in microcosm. An Aristotelian catalogue of senses, faculties, and mental activities is played against the unfolding of the infant conscience.

> Once upon a time and a very good time it was there was a moocow coming down along the road and this moocow that was down along the road met a nicens little boy named baby tuckoo. . . .
>
> His father told him that story: his father looked at him through a glass: he had a hairy face.
>
> He was baby tuckoo. The moocow came down along the road where Betty Byrne lived: she sold lemon platt.
>
> *O, the wild rose blossoms*
> *On the little green place.*
>
> He sang that song. That was his song.
>
> *O, the green wothe botheth.*
>
> When you wet the bed, first it is warm then it gets cold. His mother put on the oilsheet. That had the queer smell.

This evocation of holes in oblivion is conducted in the mode of each of the five senses in turn; hearing (the story of the moocow), sight (his father's face), taste (lemon platt), touch (warm and cold), smell (the oil-sheet). The audible soothes: the visible disturbs. Throughout Joyce's work, the senses are symbolically disposed. Smell is the means of discriminating empirical realities ("His mother had a nicer smell

than his father" is the next sentence), sight corresponds to the phantasms of oppression, hearing to the imaginative life. Touch and taste together are the modes of sex. Hearing, here, comes first, via a piece of imaginative literature. But as we can see from the vantage-point of *Finnegans Wake,* the whole book is about the encounter of baby tuckoo with the moocow: the Gripes with the mookse. (Compare the opening sentence: "Eins within a space, and a wearywide space it wast, ere wohned a Mookse," F152. Mookse is moocow plus fox plus mock turtle. The German "Eins" evokes Einstein, who presides over the interchanging of space and time; space is the Mookse's "spatialty.") The father with the hairy face is the first Mookse-avatar, the Freudian infantile analogue of God the Father.
In the *Wake*

> Derzherr, live wire, fired Benjermine Funkling outa th'Empyre, sin right hand son.

Der Erzherr (arch-lord), here a Teutonic Junker, is the God who visited his wrath on Lucifer; the hairy attribute comes through via the music-hall refrain, "There's hair, like wire, coming out of the Empire."

Dawning consciousness of his own identity ("He was baby tuckoo") leads to artistic performance ("He sang that song. That was his song.") This is hugely expanded in chapter 4:

> Now, as never before, his strange name seemed to him a prophecy . . . of the end he had been born to serve and had been following through the mists of childhood and boyhood, a symbol of the artist forging anew in his workshop out of the sluggish matter of the earth a new soaring impalpable imperishable being.

By changing the red rose to a green and dislocating the spelling, he makes the song his own ("But you could not have a green rose. But perhaps somewhere in the world you could.")

> His mother had a nicer smell than his father. She played on the piano the sailor's hornpipe for him to dance. He danced:

> *Tralala lala,*
> *Tralala tralaladdy,*

Tralala lala,
Tralala lala.

Between this innocence and its Rimbaudian recapture through the purgation of the *Wake* there is to intervene the hallucination in Circe's sty:

THE MOTHER
(*With the subtle smile of death's madness.*) I was once the beautiful May Goulding. I am dead. . . .

STEPHEN
(*Eagerly.*) Tell me the word, mother, if you know it now. The word known to all men. . . .

THE MOTHER
(*With smouldering eyes.*) Repent! O, the fire of hell!

(*Ulysses*)

This is foreshadowed as the overture to the *Portrait* closes:

He hid under the table. His mother said:
—O, Stephen will apologise.
Dante said:
—O, if not, the eagles will come and pull out his eyes.—

Pull out his eyes,
Apologise,
Apologise,
Pull out his eyes.

Apologise,
Pull out his eyes,
Pull out his eyes,
Apologise.

The eagles, eagles of Rome, are emissaries of the God with the hairy face: the punisher. They evoke Prometheus and gnawing guilt: again-bite. So the overture ends with Stephen hiding under the table awaiting the eagles. He is hiding under something most of the time: bedclothes, "the enigma of a manner," an indurated rhetoric, or some other carapace of his private world.

Theme Words

It is through their names that things have power over Stephen.

> —The language in which we are speaking is his before it
> is mine. How different are the words *home, Christ, ale,*
> *master,* on his lips and on mine! I cannot speak or write
> these words without unrest of spirit. His language, so
> familiar and so foreign, will always be for me an acquired
> speech. I have not made or accepted its words. My voice
> holds them at bay. My soul frets in the shadow of his
> language.

Not only is the Dean's English a conqueror's tongue; since the loss
of Adam's words which perfectly mirrored things, all language has
conquered the mind and imposed its own order, askew from the
order of creation. Words, like the physical world, are imposed on
Stephen from without, and it is in their canted mirrors that he
glimpses a physical and moral world already dyed the colour of his
own mind since absorbed, with language, into his personality.

> Words which he did not understand he said over and over
> to himself till he had learnt them by heart; and through
> them he had glimpses of the real world about him.

Language is a Trojan horse by which the universe gets into the mind.
The first sentence in the book isn't something Stephen sees but a
story he is told, and the overture climaxes in an insistent brainless
rhyme, its jingle corrosively fascinating to the will. It has power to
terrify a child who knows nothing of eagles, or of Prometheus, or of
how his own grownup failure to apologise will blend with gathering
blindness.

It typifies the peculiar achievement of the *Portrait* that Joyce can
cause patterns of words to make up the very moral texture of
Stephen's mind:

> Suck was a queer word. The fellow called Simon Moonan
> that name because Simon Moonan used to tie the prefect's
> false sleeves behind his back and the prefect used to let on
> to be angry. But the sound was ugly. Once he had washed
> his hands in the lavatory of the Wicklow hotel and his
> father pulled the stopper up by the chain after and the dirty

> water went down through the hole in the basin. And when
> it had all gone down slowly the hole in the basin had made
> a sound like that: suck. Only louder.
>
> To remember that and the white look of the lavatory
> made him feel cold and then hot. There were two cocks
> that you turned and the water came out: cold and hot. He
> felt cold and then a little hot: and he could see the names
> printed on the cocks. That was a very queer thing.

"Suck" joins two contexts in Stephen's mind: a playful sinner
toying with his indulgent superior, and the disappearance of dirty
water. The force of the conjunction is felt only after Stephen has
lost his sense of the reality of the forgiveness of sins in the
confessional. The habitually orthodox penitent tangles with a God
who pretends to be angry; after a reconciliation the process is
repeated. And the mark of that kind of play is disgraceful servility.
Each time the sin disappears, the sinner is mocked by an impersonal
voice out of nature: "Suck!"

This attitude to unreal good and evil furnishes a context for the
next conjunction: whiteness and coldness. Stephen finds himself, like
Simon Moonan, engaged in the rhythm of obedience to irrational
authority, bending his mind to a meaningless act, the arithmetic
contest. He is being obediently "good." And the appropriate colour
is adduced: "He thought his face must be white because it felt so
cool." (Joyce's names should always be scrutinized. Simon Moonan:
moon: the heatless [white] satellite reflecting virtue borrowed from
Simon Peter. Simony, too, is an activity naturally derived from this
casually businesslike attitude to priestly authority.)

The pallor of lunar obedient goodness is next associated with
damp repulsiveness: the limpness of a wet blanket and of a servant's
apron:

> He sat looking at the two prints of butter on his plate but
> could not eat the damp bread. The table-cloth was damp
> and limp. But he drank off the hot weak tea which the
> clumsy scullion, girt with a white apron, poured into his
> cup. He wondered whether the scullion's apron was damp
> too or whether all white things were cold and damp.

Throughout the first chapter an intrinsic linkage, white-cold-
damp-obedient, insinuates itself repeatedly. Stephen after saying his

prayers, "his shoulders shaking," so that he might not go to hell when|he died, "curled himself together under the cold white sheets, shaking and trembling. But he would not go to hell when he died, and the shaking would stop." The sea, mysterious as the terrible power of God, "was cold day and night, but it was colder at night"; we are reminded of Anna Livia's gesture of submission: "my cold father, my cold mad father, my cold mad feary father" (*Finnegans Wake*). "There was a cold night smell in the chapel. But it was a holy smell." Stephen is puzzled by the phrase in the Litany of the Blessed Virgin: Tower of Ivory. "How could a woman be a tower of ivory or a house of gold?" He ponders until the revelation comes:

> Eileen had long white hands. One evening when playing tig she had put her hands over his eyes: long and white and thin and cold and soft. That was ivory: a cold white thing. That was the meaning of *Tower of Ivory*.

This instant of insight depends on a sudden reshuffling of associations, a sudden conviction that the Mother of God, and the symbols appropriate to her, belong with the cold, the white, and the unpleasant in a blindfold morality of obedience. Contemplation focussed on language is repaid:

> *Tower of Ivory. House of Gold.* By thinking of things you could understand them.

The white-damp-obedient association reappears when Stephen is about to make his confession after the celebrated retreat; its patterns provide the language in which he thinks. Sin has been associated with fire, while the prayers of the penitents are epiphanized as "soft whispering cloudlets, soft whispering vapour, whispering and vanishing." And having been absolved:

> White pudding and eggs and sausages and cups of tea. How simple and beautiful was life after all! And life lay all before him. . . .
> The boys were all there, kneeling in their places. He knelt among them, happy and shy. The altar was heaped with fragrant masses of white flowers: and in the morning light the pale flames of the candles among the white flowers were clear and silent as his own soul.

We cannot read *Finnegans Wake* until we have realized the significance of the way the mind of Stephen Dedalus is bound in by language. He is not only an artist: he is a Dubliner.

THE PORTRAIT AS LYRIC

The "instant of emotion," of which this three-hundred-page lyric is the "simplest verbal vesture" is the exalted instant, emerging at the end of the book, of freedom, of vocation, of Stephen's destiny, winging his way above the waters at the side of the hawklike man: the instant of promise on which the crushing ironies of *Ulysses* are to fall. The epic of the sea of matter is preceded by the lyric image of a growing dream: a dream that like Richard Rowan's in *Exiles* disregards the fall of man; a dream nourished by a sensitive youth of flying above the sea into an uncreated heaven:

> The spell of arms and voices: the white arms of roads, their promise of close embraces and the black arms of tall ships that stand against the moon, their tale of distant nations. They are held out to say: We are alone—come. And the voices say with them: We are your kinsmen. And the air is thick with their company as they call to me, their kinsman, making ready to go, shaking the wings of their exultant and terrible youth.

The emotional quality of this is continuous with that of *The Count of Monte Cristo,* that fantasy of the exile returned for vengeance (the plot of the *Odyssey*) which kindled so many of Stephen's boyhood dreams:

> The figure of that dark avenger stood forth in his mind for whatever he had heard or divined in childhood of the strange and terrible. At night he built up on the parlour table an image of the wonderful island cave out of transfers and paper flowers and strips of the silver and golden paper in which chocolate is wrapped. When he had broken up this scenery, weary of its tinsel, there would come to his mind the bright picture of Marseilles, of sunny trellises and of Mercedes.

The prose surrounding Stephen's flight is empurpled with transfers and paper flowers too. It is not immature prose, as we might suppose by comparison with *Ulysses*. The prose of "The Dead" is mature prose, and "The Dead" was written in 1908. Rather, it is a meticulous pastiche of immaturity. Joyce has his eye constantly on the epic sequel.

> He wanted to meet in the real world the unsubstantial image which his soul so constantly beheld. He did not know where to seek it or how, but a premonition which led him on told him that this image would, without any overt act of his, encounter him. They would meet quietly as if they had known each other and had made their tryst, perhaps at one of the gates or in some more secret place. They would be alone, surrounded by darkness and silence: and in that moment of supreme tenderness he would be transfigured.

As the vaginal imagery of gates, secret places, and darkness implies, this is the dream that reaches temporary fulfilment in the plunge into profane love. But the ultimate "secret place" is to be Mabbot Street, outside Bella Cohen's brothel; the unsubstantial image of his quest, that of Leopold Bloom, advertisement canvasser—Monte Cristo, returned avenger, Ulysses; and the transfiguration, into the phantasmal dead son of a sentimental Jew:

> *Against the dark wall a figure appears slowly, a fairy boy of eleven, a changeling, kidnapped, dressed in an Eton suit with glass shoes and a little bronze helmet, holding a book in his hand. He reads from right to left inaudibly, smiling, kissing the page.*
> (*Ulysses*)

That Dedalus the artificer did violence to nature is the point of the epigraph from Ovid, *Et ignotas animum dimittit in artes;* the Icarian fall is inevitable.

> In tedious exile now too long detain'd
> Dedalus languish'd for his native land.
> The sea foreclos'd his flight; yet thus he said,
> Though earth and water in subjection laid,
> O cruel Minos, thy dominion be,
> We'll go through air; for sure the air is free.

> *Then to new arts his cunning thought applies,*
> *And to improve the work of nature tries.*

Stephen does not, as the careless reader may suppose, become an artist by rejecting church and country. Stephen does not become an artist at all. Country, church, and mission are an inextricable unity, and in rejecting the two that seem to hamper him, he rejects also the one on which he has set his heart. Improving the work of nature is his obvious ambition ("But you could not have a green rose. But perhaps somewhere in the world you could"), and it logically follows from the aesthetic he expounds to Lynch. It is a Neoplatonic aesthetic; the crucial principle of epiphanization has been withdrawn. He imagines that "the loveliness that has not yet come into the world" is to be found in his own soul. The earth is gross, and what it brings forth is cowdung; sound and shape and colour are "the prison gates of our soul"; and beauty is something mysteriously gestated within. The genuine artist reads signatures, the fake artist forges them, a process adumbrated in the obsession of Shem the Penman (from *Jim the Penman,* a forgotten drama about a forger) with "Macfearsome's Ossean," the most famous of literary forgeries, studying "how cutely to copy all their various styles of signature so as one day to utter an epical forged cheque on the public for his own private profit" (*Finnegans Wake*).

One can sense all this in the first four chapters of the *Portrait,* and *Ulysses* is unequivocal:

> Fabulous artificer, the hawklike man. You flew. Whereto?
> Newhaven-Dieppe, steerage passenger. Paris and back.
>
> (*Ulysses*)

The Stephen of the end of the fourth chapter, however, is still unstable; he had to be brought into a final balance, and shown at some length as a being whose development was virtually ended. Unfortunately, the last chapter makes the book a peculiarly difficult one for the reader to focus, because Joyce had to close it on a suspended chord. As a lyric, it is finished in its own terms; but the themes of the last forty pages, though they give the illusion of focussing, don't really focus until we have read well into *Ulysses.* The final chapter, which in respect to the juggernaut of *Ulysses* must be a vulnerable flank, in respect to what has gone before must be a conclusion. This problem Joyce didn't wholly solve; there remains a moral ambiguity (how seriously are we to take Stephen?) which makes the last forty pages painful reading.

Not that Stephen would stand indefinitely if *Ulysses* didn't topple him over; his equilibrium in chapter 5, though good enough to give him a sense of unusual integrity in University College, is precarious unless he can manage, in the manner of so many permanent under-graduates, to prolong the college context for the rest of his life. Each of the preceding chapters, in fact, works toward an equilibrium which is dashed when in the next chapter Stephen's world becomes larger and the frame of reference more complex. The terms of equilibrium are always stated with disquieting accuracy; at the end of chapter 1 we find:

> He was alone. He was happy and free: but he would not be anyway proud with Father Dolan. He would be very quiet and obedient: and he wished that he could do something kind for him to show him that he was not proud.

And at the end of chapter 3:

> He sat by the fire in the kitchen, not daring to speak for happiness. Till that moment he had not known how beautiful and peaceful life could be. The green square of paper pinned round the lamp cast down a tender shade. On the dresser was a plate of sausages and white pudding and on the shelf there were eggs. They would be for the breakfast in the morning after the communion in the college chapel. White pudding and eggs and sausages and cups of tea. How simple and beautiful was life after all! And life lay all before him.

Not "irony" but simply the truth: the good life conceived in terms of white pudding and sausages is unstable enough to need no underlining.

The even-numbered chapters make a sequence of a different sort. The ending of chapter 4, Stephen's panting submission to an artistic vocation:

> Evening had fallen when he woke and the sand and arid grasses of his bed glowed no longer. He rose slowly and, recalling the rapture of his sleep, sighed at its joy.

—hasn't quite the finality often read into it when the explicit parallel with the ending of chapter 2 is perceived:

> He closed his eyes, surrendering himself to her, body and mind, conscious of nothing in the world but the dark pressure of her softly parting lips. They pressed upon his brain as upon his lips as though they were the vehicle of a vague speech; and between them he felt an unknown and timid pressure, darker than the swoon of sin, softer than sound or odour.

When we link these passages with the fact that the one piece of literary composition Stephen actually achieves in the book comes out of a wet dream ("Towards dawn he awoke. O what sweet music! His soul was all dewy wet") we are in a position to see that the concluding "Welcome, O life!" has an air of finality and balance only because the diary form of the last seven pages disarms us with an illusion of auctorial impartiality.

CONTROLLING IMAGES: CLONGOWES AND BELVEDERE

Ego vs. authority is the theme of the three odd-numbered chapters, Dublin vs. the dream that of the two even-numbered ones. The generic Joyce plot, the encounter with the alter ego, is consummated when Stephen at the end of the book identifies himself with the sanctified Stephen who was stoned by the Jews after reporting a vision (Acts 7:56) and claims sonship with the classical Daedalus who evaded the ruler of land and sea by turning his soul to obscure arts. The episodes are built about adumbrations of this encounter: with Father Conmee, with Monte Cristo, with the whores, with the broad-shouldered moustached student who cut the word "Foetus" in a desk, with the weary mild confessor, with the bird-girl. Through this repeated plot intertwine controlling emotions and controlling images that mount in complexity as the book proceeds.

In chapter 1 the controlling emotion is fear, and the dominant image Father Dolan and his pandybat; this, associated with the hangman-god and the priestly denial of the senses, was to become one of Joyce's standard images for Irish clericalism—hence the jack-in-the-box appearance of Father Dolan in Circe's nightmare imbroglio, his pandybat cracking twice like thunder (*Ulysses*). Stephen's comment, in the mode of Blake's repudiation of the God who slaughtered Jesus, emphasizes the inclusiveness of the image: "I never could read His handwriting except His criminal thumbprint on the haddock."

Chapter 2 opens with a triple image of Dublin's prepossessions: music, sport, religion. The first is exhibited via Uncle Charles singing sentimental ballads in the outhouse; the second via Stephen's ritual run around the park under the eye of a superannuated trainer, which his uncle enjoins on him as the whole duty of a Dubliner; the third via the clumsy piety of Uncle Charles, kneeling on a red handkerchief and reading above his breath "from a thumb-blackened prayerbook wherein catchwords were printed at the foot of every page." This trinity of themes is unwound and entwined throughout the chapter, like a net woven round Stephen; it underlies the central incident, the Whitsuntide play in the Belvedere chapel (religion), which opens with a display by the dumbbell team (sport) preluded by sentimental waltzes from the soldier's band (music).

While he is waiting to play his part, Stephen is taunted by fellow-students, who rally him on a fancied love affair and smiting his calf with a cane bid him recite the *Confiteor*. His mind goes back to an analogous incident, when a similar punishment had been visited on his refusal to "admit that Byron was no good." The further analogy with Father Dolan is obvious; love, art, and personal independence are thus united in an ideogram of the prepossessions Stephen is determined to cultivate in the teeth of persecution.

The dream-world Stephen nourishes within himself is played against manifestations of music, sport, and religion throughout the chapter. The constant ironic clash of Dublin vs. the Dream animates chapter 2, as the clash of the ego vs. authority did chapter 1. All these themes come to focus during Stephen's visit with his father to Cork. The dream of rebellion he has silently cultivated is externalized by the discovery of the word "Foetus" carved in a desk by a forgotten medical student:

> It shocked him to find in the outer world a trace of what he had deemed till then a brutish and individual malady of his own mind. His monstrous reveries came thronging into his memory. They too had sprung up before him, suddenly and furiously, out of mere words.

The possibility of shame gaining the upper hand is dashed, however, by the sudden banal intrusion of his father's conversation

("When you kick out for yourself, Stephen, as I daresay you will one of these days, remember, whatever you do, to mix with gentlemen"). Against the standards of Dublin his monstrous reveries acquire a Satanic glamour, and the trauma is slowly diverted into a resolution to rebel. After his father has expressed a resolve to "leave him to his Maker" (religion), and offered to "sing a tenor song against him" (music) or "vault a fivebarred gate against him" (sport), Stephen muses, watching his father and two cronies drinking to the memory of their past:

> An abyss of fortune or of temperament sundered him from them. His mind seemed older than theirs: it shone coldly on their strifes and happiness and regrets like a moon upon a younger earth. No life or youth stirred in him as it had stirred in them. He had known neither the pleasure of companionship with others nor the vigour of rude male health nor filial piety. Nothing stirred within his soul but a cold and cruel and loveless lust.

After one final effort to compromise with Dublin on Dublin's terms has collapsed into futility ("The pot of pink enamel paint gave out and the wainscot of his bedroom remained with its unfinished and illplastered coat"), he fiercely cultivates his rebellious thoughts, and moving by day and night "among distorted images of the outer world," plunges at last into the arms of whores. "The holy encounter he had then imagined at which weakness and timidity and inexperience were to fall from him," finally arrives in inversion of Father Dolan's and Uncle Charles's religion: his descent into night-town is accompanied by lurid evocations of a Black Mass (cf. *Ulysses*):

> The yellow gasflames arose before his troubled vision against the vapoury sky, burning as if before an altar. Before the doors and in the lighted halls groups were gathered arrayed as for some rite. He was in another world: he had awakened from a slumber of centuries.

CONTROLLING IMAGES: SIN AND REPENTANCE

Each chapter in the *Portrait* gathers up the thematic material of the preceding ones and entwines them with a dominant theme of its own. In chapter 3 the fear-pandybat motif is present in Father

Arnall's crudely materialistic hell, of which even the thickness of the walls is specified; and the Dublin-vs.-dream motif has ironic inflections in Stephen's terror-stricken broodings, when the dream has been twisted into a dream of holiness, and even Dublin appears transfigured:

> How beautiful must be a soul in the state of grace when God looked upon it with love!
>
> Frowsy girls sat along the curbstones before their baskets. Their dank hair trailed over their brows. They were not beautiful to see as they crouched in the mire. But their souls were seen by God; and if their souls were in a state of grace they were radiant to see; and God loved them, seeing them.

A rapprochement in these terms between the outer world and Stephen's desires is too inadequate to need commentary; and it makes vivid as nothing else could the hopeless inversion of his attempted self-sufficiency. It underlines, in yet another way, his persistent sin: and the dominant theme of chapter 3 is Sin. A fugue-like opening plays upon the Seven Deadly Sins in turn; gluttony is in the first paragraph ("Stuff it into you, his belly counselled him"), followed by lust, then sloth ("A cold lucid indifference reigned in his soul"), pride ("His pride in his own sin, his loveless awe of God, told him that his offence was too grievous to be atoned for"), anger ("The blundering answer stirred the embers of his contempt for his fellows"); finally, a recapitulation fixes each term of the mortal catalogue in a phrase, enumerating how "from the evil seed of lust all the other deadly sins had sprung forth."

Priest and punisher inhabit Stephen himself as well as Dublin: when he is deepest in sin he is most thoroughly a theologian. A paragraph of gloomy introspection is juxtaposed with a list of theological questions that puzzle Stephen's mind as he awaits the preacher:

> Is baptism with mineral water valid? How comes it that while the first beatitude promises the kingdom of heaven to the poor of heart, the second beatitude promises also to the meek that they shall possess the land? . . . If the wine change into vinegar and the host crumble into corruption

after they have been consecrated, is Jesus Christ still
present under their species as God and as man?

—Here he is! Here he is!

A boy from his post at the window had seen the rector
come from the house. All the catechisms were opened and
all heads bent upon them silently.

Wine changed into vinegar and the host crumbled into corruption
fits exactly the Irish clergy of "a church which was the scullery-maid
of Christendom." The excited "Here he is! Here he is!" following
hard on the mention of Jesus Christ and signalling nothing more
portentous than the rector makes the point as dramatically as
anything in the book, and the clinching sentence, with the students
suddenly bending over their catechisms, places the rector as the
vehicle of pandybat morality.

The last of the theological questions is the telling question. Stephen never expresses doubt of the existence of God nor of the essential
validity of the priestly office—his *Non serviam* is not a *non credo,* and
he talks of a "malevolent reality" behind these appearances—but the
wine and bread that were offered for his veneration were changed into
vinegar and crumbled into corruption. And it was the knowledge of
that underlying validity clashing with his refusal to do homage to
vinegar and rot that evoked his ambivalent poise of egocentric despair.
The hell of Father Arnall's sermon, so emotionally overwhelming, so
picayune beside the horrors that Stephen's imagination can generate,
had no more ontological content for Stephen than had "an eternity of
bliss in the company of the dean of studies."

The conflict of this central chapter is again between the phantasmal and the real. What is real—psychologically real, because
realized—is Stephen's anguish and remorse, and its context in the life
of the flesh. What is phantasmal is the "heaven" of the Church and
the "good life" of the priest. It is only fear that makes him clutch
after the latter at all; his reaching out after orthodox salvation is, as
we have come to expect, presented in terms that judge it:

> The wind blew over him and passed on to the myriads and
> myriads of other souls, on whom God's favour shone now
> more and now less, stars now brighter and now dimmer,
> sustained and failing. And the glimmering souls passed
> away, sustained and failing, merged in a moving breath.
> One soul was lost; a tiny soul; his. It flickered once and

went out, forgotten, lost. The end: black cold void waste.

Consciousness of place came ebbing back to him slowly over a vast tract of time unlit, unfelt, unlived. The squalid scene composed itself around him; the common accents, the burning gasjets in the shops, odours of fish and spirits and wet sawdust, moving men and women. An old woman was about to cross the street, an oilcan in her hand. He bent down and asked her was there a chapel near.

That wan waste world of flickering stars is the best Stephen has been able to do towards an imaginative grasp of the communion of Saints sustained by God; "unlit, unfelt, unlived" explains succinctly why it had so little hold on him, once fear had relaxed. Equally pertinent is the vision of human temporal occupations the sermon evokes:

What did it profit a man to gain the whole world if he lost his soul? At last he had understood: and human life lay around him, a plain of peace whereon antlike men laboured in brotherhood, their dead sleeping under quiet mounds.

To maintain the life of grace in the midst of nature, sustained by so cramped a vision of the life of nature, would mean maintaining an intolerable tension. Stephen's unrelenting philosophic bias, his determination to understand what he is about, precludes his adopting the double standard of the Dubliners; to live both the life of nature and the life of grace he must enjoy an imaginative grasp of their relationship which stunts neither. "No one doth well against his will," writes Saint Augustine, "even though what he doth, be well"; and Stephen's will is firmly harnessed to his understanding. And there is no one in Dublin to help him achieve understanding. Father Arnall's sermon precludes rather then secures a desirable outcome, for it follows the modes of pandybat morality and Dublin materiality. Its only possible effect on Stephen is to lash his dormant conscience into a frenzy. The description of Hell as "a strait and dark and foul smelling prison, an abode of demons and lost souls, filled with fire and smoke," with walls four thousand miles thick, its damned packed in so tightly that "they are not even able to remove from the eye the worm that gnaws it," is childishly grotesque beneath its sweeping eloquence; and the hair-splitting catalogues of pains—pain of loss, pain of conscience (divided into three heads), pain of extension, pain of intensity, pain of eternity—is cast in a brainlessly analytic mode that effectively prevents any corresponding Heaven from possessing any reality at all.

Stephen's unstable pact with the Church, and its dissolution, follows the pattern of composition and dissipation established by his other dreams: the dream for example of the tryst with "Mercedes," which found ironic reality among harlots. It parallels exactly his earlier attempt to "build a breakwater of order and elegance against the sordid tide of life without him," whose failure, with the exhaustion of his money, was epiphanized in the running dry of a pot of pink enamel paint. His regimen at that time:

> He bought presents for everyone, overhauled his rooms, wrote out resolutions, marshalled his books up and down their shelves, pored over all kinds of price lists

is mirrored by his searching after spiritual improvement:

> His daily life was laid out in devotional areas. By means of ejaculations and prayers he stored up ungrudgingly for the souls in purgatory centuries of days and quarantines and years. . . . He offered up each of his three daily chaplets that his soul might grow strong in each of the three theological virtues. . . . On each of the seven days of the week he further prayed that one of the seven gifts of the Holy Ghost might descend upon his soul.

The "loan bank" he had opened for the family, out of which he had pressed loans on willing borrowers "that he might have the pleasure of making out receipts and reckoning the interests on sums lent" finds its counterpart in the benefits he stored up for souls in purgatory that he might enjoy the spiritual triumph of "achieving with ease so many fabulous ages of canonical penances." Both projects are parodies on the doctrine of economy of grace; both are attempts, corrupted by motivating self-interest, to make peace with Dublin on Dublin's own terms; and both are short-lived.

As this precise analogical structure suggests, the action of each of the five chapters is really the same action. Each chapter closes with a synthesis of triumph which the next destroys. The triumph of the appeal to Father Conmee from lower authority, of the appeal to the harlots from Dublin, of the appeal to the Church from sin, of the appeal to art from the priesthood (the bird-girl instead of the Virgin) is always the same triumph raised to a more comprehensive level. It is an attempt to find new parents; new fathers in the odd chapters, new objects of love in the even. The last version of Father Conmee is the "priest of the eternal imagination"; the last version of Mercedes is the "lure of the fallen seraphim." But the last version of the mother who said, "O, Stephen will apologise" is the mother who prays on the last page "that I may learn in my own life and away from home and friends what the heart is and what it feels." The mother remains.

THE DOUBLE FEMALE

As in *Dubliners* and *Exiles,* the female role in the *Portrait* is less to arouse than to elucidate masculine desires. Hence the complex function in the book of physical love: the physical is the analogue of the spiritual, as St. Augustine insisted in his *Confessions* (which, with Ibsen's *Brand,* is the chief archetype of Joyce's book). The poles between which this affection moves are those of St. Augustine and St. John: the Whore of Babylon and the Bride of Christ. The relation between the two is far from simple, and Stephen moves in a constant tension between them.

His desire, figured in the visions of Monte Cristo's Mercedes, "to meet in the real world the unsubstantial image which his soul so constantly beheld," draws him toward the prostitute ("In her arms he felt that he had suddenly become strong and fearless and sure of himself") and simultaneously toward the vaguely spiritual satisfaction represented with equal vagueness by the wraithlike E———— C————, to whom he twice writes verses. The Emma Clery of *Stephen Hero,* with her loud forced manners and her body compact of pleasure, was refined into a wraith with a pair of initials to parallel an intangible Church. She is continually assimilated to the image of the Blessed Virgin and of the heavenly Bride. The torture she costs him is the torture his apostasy costs him. His flirtation with her is his flirtation with Christ. His profane villanelle draws its imagery from religion—the incense, the eucharistic hymn, the chalice—and her heart, following Dante's image, is a rose, and in her praise "the earth was like a swinging swaying censer, a ball of incense."

The woman is the Church. His vision of greeting Mercedes with "a sadly proud gesture of refusal":

—Madam, I never eat muscatel grapes.

is fulfilled when he refuses his Easter communion. Emma's eyes, in their one explicit encounter, speak to him from beneath a cowl, "The glories of Mary held his soul captive," and a temporary reconciliation of his lust and his spiritual thirst is achieved as he reads the Lesson out of the Song of Solomon. In the midst of his repentance she functions as imagined mediator: "The image of Emma appeared before him," and, repenting, "he imagined that he stood near Emma in a wide land, and, humbly and in tears, bent and kissed the elbow of her sleeve." Like Dante's Beatrice, she manifests in his earthly experience the Church Triumphant of his spiritual dream. And when he rejects her because she seems to be flirting with Father Moran, his anger is couched in the anticlerical terms of his apostasy: "He had done well to leave her to flirt with her priest, to toy with a church which was the scullery-maid of Christendom."

That Kathleen ni Houlihan can flirt with priests is the unforgivable sin underlying Stephen's rejection of Ireland. But he makes a clear distinction between the stupid clericalism which makes intellectual and communal life impossible, and his long-nourished vision of an artist's Church Triumphant upon earth. He rejects the actual for daring to fall short of his vision.

THE FINAL BALANCE

The climax of the book is of course Stephen's ecstatic discovery of his vocation at the end of chapter 4. The prose rises in nervous excitement to beat again and again the tambours of a fin-de-siècle ecstasy:

His heart trembled; his breath came faster and a wild spirit passed over his limbs as though he were soaring sunward. His heart trembled in an ecstasy of fear and his soul was in flight. His soul was soaring in an air beyond the world and the body he knew was purified in a breath and delivered of incertitude and made radiant and commingled with the element of the spirit. An ecstasy of flight made radiant his eyes and wild his breath and tremulous and wild and radiant his windswept limbs.

—One! Two! . . . Look out!—
—O, Cripes, I'm drownded!

The interjecting voices of course are those of bathers, but their ironic appropriateness to Stephen's Icarian "soaring sunward" is not meant to escape us: divers have their own "ecstasy of flight," and Icarus was "drownded." The imagery of Stephen's ecstasy is fetched from many sources; we recognize Shelley's skylark, Icarus, the glorified body of the Resurrection (cf. "His soul had arisen from the grave of boyhood, spurning her graveclothes") and a tremulousness from which it is difficult to dissociate adolescent sexual dreams (which the Freudians tell us are frequently dreams of flying). The entire eight-page passage is cunningly organized with great variety of rhetoric and incident; but we cannot help noticing the limits set on vocabulary and figures of thought. The empurpled triteness of such a cadence as "radiant his eyes and wild his breath and tremulous and wild and radiant his windswept face" is enforced by recurrence: "But her long fair hair was girlish: and girlish, and touched with the wonder of mortal beauty, her face." "Ecstasy" is the keyword, indeed. This riot of feelings corresponds to no vocation definable in mature terms; the paragraphs come to rest on images of irresponsible motion:

> He turned away from her suddenly and set off across the strand. His cheeks were aflame; his body was aglow; his limbs were trembling. On and on and on and on he strode, far out over the sands, singing wildly to the sea, crying to greet the advent of the life that had cried to him.

What "life" connotes it skills not to ask; the word recurs and recurs. So does the motion onward and onward and onward:

> A wild angel had appeared to him, the angel of mortal youth and beauty, an envoy from the fair courts of life, to throw open before him in an instant of ecstasy the gates of all the ways of error and glory. On and on and on and on!

It may be well to recall Joyce's account of the romantic temper:

> an insecure, unsatisfied, impatient temper which sees no fit abode here for its ideals and chooses therefore to behold them under insensible figures. As a result of this choice it comes to disregard certain limitations. Its figures are blown to wild adventures, lacking the gravity of solid bodies.
>
> (*Stephen Hero*)

Joyce also called *Prometheus Unbound* "the Schwärmerei of a young jew."

And it is quite plain from the final chapter of the *Portrait* that we are not to accept the mode of Stephen's "freedom" as the "message" of the book. The "priest of the eternal imagination" turns out to be indigestibly Byronic. Nothing is more obvious than his total lack of humour. The dark intensity of the first four chapters is moving enough, but our impulse on being confronted with the final edition of Stephen Dedalus is to laugh; and laugh at this moment we dare not; he is after all a victim being prepared for a sacrifice. His shape, as Joyce said, can no longer change. The art he has elected is not "the slow elaborative patience of the art of satisfaction." "On and on and on and on" will be its inescapable mode. He does not *see* the girl who symbolizes the full revelation; "she seemed like one whom magic had changed into the likeness of a strange and beautiful seabird," and he confusedly apprehends a sequence of downy and feathery incantations. What, in the last chapter, he does see he sees only to reject, in favour of an incantatory "loveliness which has not yet come into the world."

The only creative attitude to language exemplified in the book is that of Stephen's father:

> —Is it Christy? he said. There's more cunning in one
> of those warts on his bald head than in a pack of jack foxes.

His vitality is established before the book is thirty pages under way. Stephen, however, isn't enchanted at any time by the proximity of such talk. He isn't, as a matter of fact, even interested in it. Without a backward glance, he exchanges this father for a myth.

A Portrait of the Artist as Friend

Richard Ellmann

Revolutionaries fatten on opposition but grow thin and pale when treated with indulgence. Joyce's ostracism from Dublin lacked, as he was well aware, the moral decisiveness of Dante's exile from Florence in that Joyce kept the keys to the gate. He was neither bidden to leave nor forbidden to return, and he did in fact go back four times. But whenever his relations with his native land seemed in danger of improving, he found a new incident to solidify his intransigence and reaffirm the rightness of his voluntary exile. He even showed some grand resentment at the possibility of Irish independence on the grounds that it would change the relationship he had so carefully established between himself and his country. "Should I," he asked someone, "wish to alter the conditions that have made me what I am?" At first he thought only his soul was in danger in Ireland. Then, when his difficulties over the publication of *Dubliners* became so great, he thought his writing career was being deliberately conspired against. Finally he came to assert that he was physically in danger. This suspicion began when his wife paid a visit to Galway in 1922. Civil war had just broken out in the west, and her train was fired on by soldiers. Joyce chose to believe that the bullets were really aimed at him, and afterwards refused to return to Ireland because he said he feared for his life. That Joyce could not have written his books in Ireland is likely enough, but he felt the need for maintaining his intimacy with his country by

From *The Kenyon Review* 18, no. 1 (Winter 1956). © 1956 by Kenyon College.

continually renewing the quarrel with her which prompted his first departure.

In his books too his heroes are outcasts in one way or another, and much of their interest lies in why they are cast out and by whom. Are they "self-doomed," as Joyce says of himself in his broadside, "The Holy Office," or are they doomed by society? To the extent that the hero is himself responsible, he is Faustlike, struggling like Stephen Dedalus or Richard Rowan to achieve a freedom beyond human power. To the extent that society is responsible he is Christlike, a sacrificial victim whose sufferings torment his tormentors. Joyce was not so masochistic as to identify himself completely with the helpless victim; at the very moment he attacks society most bitterly as his oppressor, he will not completely deny the authorship of his own despair. Like the boy in the ballad of the Jew's daughter, he is immolated, *consenting*. Again he was not so possessed with self as to adopt utterly the part of the anarchic individual. He carefully avoids making his heroes anything but unhappy in their triumphant self-righteousness.

Half-willing and half-forced to be a sufferer, Stephen endows the artist in *A Portrait of the Artist as a Young Man* with a rather similar mixture of qualities, the total power of a god bored by his own handiwork and the heroic impotence of a Lucifer, smarting from pain which he has chosen to bear. To be both god and devil is perhaps to be man. In *Ulysses* the paradoxes ascribed to these forces are the paradoxes of being Joyce: God begets Himself, sends Himself between Himself and others, is put upon by His own friends. Joyce and Stephen challenge in the same way the forces which they have brought into being. As Stephen says of Shakespeare, "His unremitting intellect is the hornmad Iago ceaselessly willing that the moor in him shall suffer." If the residents of heaven were not androgynous, he says, God would be bawd and cuckold too, arranging for his own humiliation with his own creatures.

In his books Joyce represents heroes who seek freedom, which is also exile, voluntarily and by compulsion. The question of ultimate responsibility is raised and then dropped without an answer. Joyce's hero is as lonely as Byron's; consequently Joyce obliterated Stephen's brother, Maurice, from the *Portrait* after using him tentatively in *Stephen Hero,* for there must be no adherent, and the home must be a rallying-point of betrayal. A cluster of themes—the sacrilege of Faust, the suffering of Christ, the exile of Dante—reach a focus in the problem of friendship. For if friendship exists, it impugns the quality of exile and of lonely heroism. If the world is not altogether hostile, we may forgive it for having mistreated us, and so be forced into the false position of warriors without adversaries. Joyce allows his hero to sample friendship before discovering its flaws, and then with the theme of broken friendship represents his hero's broken ties with Ireland and the world.

The friendship is invariably between men; here Joyce is very much the Dubliner. A curious aspect of Irish life is that relationships between men seem more vital there than relationships between men and women. It is not easy to know whether this trait is due to a misogynistic bias in Irish Catholicism, or, less impressively, to long hours of pub crawling. Whatever the cause, the trait carries over into the work of Joyce. In his writings there is a succession of important friendships between men which receive more of his attention than love affairs. He displays a man's world, in which Emma, Gretta, Bertha, Molly, Anna, and Isabel occupy, however fetchingly, only a bed or a kitchen. Frank Budgen describes a number of Joyce's diatribes against women who venture beyond their station. Once he remonstrated with Joyce a little, saying, "But as I remember you in other days, you always fell back upon the fact that woman's flesh was provoking and desirable, whatever else was objectionable about her." Joyce snorted and replied, "Perhaps I did. Now I don't care a damn about their bodies. I am only interested in their clothes." In his books the men, whether lovers or husbands, are almost always away from home, drinking in a pub, talking on the library steps, walking in Phoenix Park or along the strand. Joyce remarked to his friend Ottocaro Weiss, in explanation of his principles of dramaturgy, "When things get slow, bring a woman on the stage." Women appear brilliantly in his work, but they are admitted only on condition that they remain bright accessories to the main struggles.

To isolate the male friendships in Joyce's novels does not, of course, give a complete account of the novels; but it does them surprisingly little violence. Each book has a special view of friendship, although later developments are lightly prefigured in the earliest, *Stephen Hero*. Here Joyce touches upon Stephen's amorous interest in Emma Clery, but shows his relation to her as wary and circumspect when it is not merely blunt. The main interest attaches however to his friendship with Cranly, which is much more tender and complex. Cranly's alienation from Stephen is the novel's principal dramatic action; three explanations of it are given, none of them wholly satisfactory. Stanislaus Joyce has commented that his brother was baffled by the behavior of Cranly's prototype, J. F. Byrne, and this bafflement may account for the various interpretations of it offered in *Stephen Hero*. The first reason is suggested to Stephen by his brother Maurice. "Cranly," he says, "wants to become more and more necessary to you until he can have you in his power." Stephen repudiates this analysis, which he contends is based upon a novel conception of friendship. But it is never discredited. The second reason appears on the surface to be an aesthetic disagreement, Cranly's cool reception of Stephen's paper on "Drama and Life." The first blood between them is this partial rejection of one of Stephen's literary works. Joyce's own ruptures with good friends often came about in the same way. A chill developed between him and Wyndham Lewis after *Time and Western Man* had criticized Joyce's work, and Joyce had little more to do with Ezra Pound, in spite of all Pound had previously done for Joyce, after Pound expressed his disapproval of the early sections of *Finnegans Wake*. Like many authors, Joyce always preferred to suspect that literary disagreement with him arose from personal causes, not detached intellectual judgment. When Jung wrote his critique of *Ulysses*, Joyce's comment was, "What does Jung have against me? Why does he dislike me? I haven't even met him."

Cranly's conflict with Stephen becomes more earnest when he follows his refusal of sympathy for Stephen's paper with a refusal of sympathy for Stephen's detachment towards his dying sister Isobel. Joyce too was capable of showing this utter detachment, and in later life he brought on a quarrel with Paul Léon by remarking casually of Lucia Joyce's mental collapse that it was like a story in *Dubliners*. Léon accused him of cerebralizing tragedy. It may be that Cranly's judgments of Stephen are well founded, but we are never allowed to regard them so. They at once make Stephen suspicious of Cranly's attitude towards him. Joyce writes in a passage unconsciously full of adolescent egoism, "He fancied moreover that he detected in Cranly's attitude towards him a certain hostility, arising out of a thwarted desire to imitate. Cranly was fond of ridiculing Stephen to his bar companions and though this was supposed to be no more than banter Stephen found touches of seriousness in it." He goes on a little pompously, "Stephen refused to close with this trivial falsehood of his friend and continued to share all the secrets of his bosom as if he had not observed any change. He no longer, however, sought his friend's opinion or allowed the sour dissatisfaction of his friend's mood to weigh with him." Like the desire to possess, suggested by Maurice, Stephen's second diagnosis, "the thwarted desire to imitate," is self-engrossed.

The third reason is more complicated, for it involves another person. Stephen's beloved, Emma Clery, walks by the two young men, and when they bow to her she disregards Stephen to bow only to Cranly. To Cranly's question, "Why did she do that?" Stephen replies with a laugh, "An invitation perhaps." He pretends to regard the incident lightly, but sexual rivalry and jealousy seem bound to divide the two young men more decisively than the desire of Cranly to dominate or imitate Stephen. One of the main functions of female characters in Joyce is to promote division between male friends. Yet Cranly's liking for Emma is an implied compliment to Stephen's taste in women, and all three reasons, the desire to dominate and emulate and steal away his friend's girl, have in common the fact that it is Cranly who takes the first steps towards enmity, and that all explanations of his behavior are essentially proofs of his dependence upon Stephen. Cranly's feelings are reactions to Stephen's feelings.

In *A Portrait of the Artist as a Young Man* the themes introduced in *Stephen Hero* are heightened by the new unifying theme of artistic development. Friendship too is viewed with greater intensity, its collisions are more serious, and at the end of the book it begins to seem an impossibility. In later life Joyce remarked to Samuel Beckett, "I don't love anyone but my family," in a tone that implied that he did not really *like* anyone but his family either. The *Portrait* justifies the hero's renunciation of friendship more elaborately than *Stephen Hero* attempted to do. While Stephen has another important friendship, with Lynch, Cranly remains his chief confidant. He talks to Lynch about aesthetics, Lynch's coarse responses providing a ground bass for his tenor, but he talks to Cranly about his secret thoughts.

So the resolution of the book's problem, which is what Stephen should do next, comes in a climactic discussion with Cranly. What in *Stephen Hero* was only a suspicion becomes here a virtual certainty. Stephen asks Cranly to come and talk with him, but Cranly delays. During the delay Emma Clery passes by, and again bows across Stephen in response to Cranly's greeting. Stephen is affronted and pounces on this deliberate misdirection of her favor. "Was there not a slight flush on Cranly's cheek?" he asks himself. "Did that explain his friend's listless silence, his harsh comments, the sudden intrusions of rude speech with which he had shattered so often Stephen's ardent wayward confessions?" In the subsequent conversation, Cranly suspiciously takes the part of mothers and of women generally; he accuses Stephen of inability to love. It is this conversation which determines Stephen upon departure, for it makes him feel that he cannot hope for friendship: "Away then; it is time to go. . . . His friendship was coming to an end. Yes; he would go. He could not strive against another. He knew his part."

But to give Stephen more complete mastery of the situation, Joyce adds an element not present in *Stephen Hero*. This too occurs in the final conversation. Cranly reminds Stephen that he will be alone, "And you know what that word means? Not only to be separated from all others but to have not even one friend. . . . And not to have any one person . . . who would be more than a friend, more even than the noblest and truest friend a man ever had." Stephen looks at him and wonders if he has spoken to himself. "Of whom are you speaking?" he asks at last, and receives no answer. The effect of the suggestion is to bring Cranly's emotions even more completely within Stephen's circle of attraction. His attachment to Stephen and to Stephen's girl are presumably related, but Joyce does not labor the relation. In the last pages of the book Stephen writes in his journal of Cranly's growing intimacy with Emma, "Is he the shining light now? If so, I swear it was I who discovered him." The artist discovers his own rival, shapes him even for the task of betraying him.

The self-centered character of the *Portrait* precludes Joyce's enlarging upon Stephen's further relations with Cranly. Stephen dispenses with both love and friendship, reluctantly but with what he considers justification. The contest of love and hate between him and Cranly is irrelevant except in so far as it compels his departure to search for freedom. The only question is how long it will take Stephen to slough off both Cranly and Emma. The *Portrait* ends in exile for one; Joyce might have ended it with exile for two, with a departure modeled upon his own setting forth with Nora Barnacle in 1904; but he wished Stephen at this stage to find no one to help him. Stephen's self-isolation is heroic but presumptuous, suited as Stanislaus Joyce says to his character as Irish Faust. On the other hand, his refusal to strive against another, his endurance of gratuitous deceit, gives him also a Christlike character.

Joyce reserved for his play *Exiles* a saturnalia of the emotions of friendship. By 1914, when he began the play, he had had a series of important experiences with friends which he had not had in 1902, the last year to which his earlier books refer. The first came on his return from Paris in 1903. He had written of sexual exploits in Paris to his friend Vincent Cosgrave, the prototype of Lynch. He did so in contravention of the advice of Cranly's prototype, J. F. Byrne, who thought Cosgrave vicious, and later had his judgment confirmed. When Joyce returned to Dublin, Byrne demanded an explanation for Joyce's having flouted his advice, and when Joyce could not furnish an adequate one Byrne broke off with him. In *Ulysses* Stephen says of Cranly, "He now will leave me. As I am. All or not at all." Actually they became friends again, but Joyce has Stephen decide that Cranly's protectiveness is an attempt to keep him to himself.

A second experience that entered into *Exiles* occurred in 1909 when Joyce was making a brief visit to Dublin. He called on Cosgrave and to his consternation heard Cosgrave boast that he had seduced Nora Barnacle after her supposed allegiance to Joyce began. Joyce went in despair to Byrne, then living at 7 Eccles Street, and told him what he had just heard. He wrote home to Nora in such agony and with so much recrimination that his distressed wife showed the letters to Stanislaus Joyce. Fortunately Stanislaus was able to prove to his brother that Cosgrave was lying, because five years before Cosgrave had confidentially confessed to Stanislaus at a pub his failure with Nora. If the relationship with Byrne seemed to argue possessiveness, that with Cosgrave led Joyce to see in friendship an aspect of hatred and treachery. The relationship of man and woman is bewilderingly precarious here. When Joyce's faith in Nora was shaken, he appears to have made no attempt to defend her or to heed her defense. (His attitude had not yet attained the sangfroid of Wellington in the first chapter of *Finnegans Wake,* who, in another treatment of Joyce's theme, on receiving Napoleon's message, "Fieldgaze thy tiny frow [wife]. Hugacting. Nap." replies "Figtreeyou!") Nora had to be vindicated by someone else, and that one a man; otherwise no vindication would seem to have been possible. Joyce was unhappily quick to suspect treachery in those closest to him. At a word, his friend is a Judas, his wife a Delilah.

A third episode occurred in Trieste, when an Italian friend of Joyce, who was also an admirer of Nora, seemed to Joyce to be as much drawn to himself as to her. Little is known about this relationship, but it is probable that it reinforced his conception of the homosexual undercurrent in friendship. Finally, Joyce paid a visit to Dr. Oliver Gogarty in Dublin in 1912, and from Gogarty's account this ended in mutual hostility. From these four episodes Joyce drew the picture of friendship which appears in *Exiles,* where your friend is someone who wants to possess you mentally and your wife physically, and longs to prove himself your disciple by betraying you.

Joyce focuses attention in the play upon husband rather than upon lover. In the notes to *Exiles* he attributes to the newly published pages of *Madame Bovary* (discarded by Flaubert) the current movement in thought which takes more interest in the husband's dilemma than the lover's glamor. But principally the husband-hero was a figure through whom he could keep his own matured *persona* as the center. In his university days Joyce denounced *Othello,* and while we do not know the reasons we can guess that he already repudiated the naiveté and easy susceptibility of the hero. His own role with Cosgrave was equally undistinguished, but in the play he makes Richard a more powerful antagonist for Robert than Othello is for Iago. The two men watch each other in what Joyce called three cat-and-mouse acts, with Richard's mistress-wife as the prize for the more feline.

As always, the hero's motivation cuts two ways. On the primary level Richard desires that his wife share in his own Faustian freedom; he would like, but cannot ask, that her freedom should result in fidelity. On the secondary level he longs to be wronged by her and by his best friend, so as to feel vicariously the thrill of adultery. Her infidelity and Robert's will confirm his view of the impossibility of a genuine tie between people; yet in his partial wish for this confirmation he is an accomplice in the infidelity. As for Robert, his motivation is simpler: he wishes to possess Bertha, and also to possess and dominate Richard through the body of his wife. Richard is caught in his two conceptions of himself; as Faust searching for freedom he cannot try to control another, as Christ he cannot resist for himself. There is also another element, his love for his wife, to keep him from acting. For Bertha love is not what it is to Richard; rather than the bestowal of freedom, it is the insistence upon bonds. She waits for the sign which he will not give, and encourages Robert less for himself than in the hope of bestirring her husband to express his love. Richard has begotten the situation from which he proceeds to suffer.

The winner of the bout is not decided. Joyce asked Paul Suter, a friend in Zurich, whether he thought Bertha was unfaithful to Richard or not, and Suter sensed so much agitation beneath the question that he evaded answering it. Yet there can be no doubt that Robert feels he has lost, and that Richard retains his moral ascendancy. Whatever happens between the bodies of Robert and Bertha, their beings are completely dominated by Richard. "There is a faith still stranger than the faith of the disciple in his master," says Richard to Robert, "the faith of a master in the disciple who will betray him."

In *Ulysses* betrayal serves as a countertheme to the main action, which is the coming together of Bloom and Stephen. When Mulligan takes Stephen's arm, Stephen says to himself, "Cranly's arm. His arm," as if they were equally unreliable. The crime of friendship in *Ulysses*, committed by Mulligan, Lynch, and Cranly ("He now will leave me"), is the crime of leaving one's friend in the lurch. For this Stephen calls Lynch a Judas and predicts he will hang himself. Incidentally, as if to confirm Joyce's view, Cosgrave did commit suicide in the late 1920s. The sexual betrayal theme is presented ingeniously in Stephen's description of Shakespeare, with whom both he and Bloom are somewhat identified; Shakespeare, Stephen holds, was betrayed by his brother with his wife, and betrayed with the dark lady of the sonnets by his "dearmylove," that is, by Mr. W. H., for whom he had a homosexual affection.

Among all these betrayals of one man by another, the relationship of Bloom and Stephen stands forth in vivid contrast. Mulligan suspects that Bloom's interest in Stephen is homosexual, but the suspicion is only malicious. The relationship of the two is not friendly, but paternal and filial. Joyce seems to imply that only within the family, or the pseudo-family, can a solid bond be established. Even this relationship has its sexual content, for Bloom, in his desire to play the role of father with Stephen and to have him for son is motivated also by jealousy of Blazes Boylan and by a desire to free his wife from Boylan's embraces. Consequently, like Stephen's God and Stephen's Shakespeare, Bloom is bawd and cuckold, showing Stephen a picture of Molly in an alluring costume. It cannot be wholly irrelevant that Joyce himself sent a picture of Nora to Forrest Reid in 1918, shortly before he wrote this episode. Bloom continues his invitation by asking Stephen to give Molly lessons in Italian in exchange for lessons in singing. The relationship with another man is so important to him that it reduces the importance of his relationship with a woman.

The treatment of Bloom and Stephen finds no parallel in the earlier novels, but it recalls the theme of the story "The Dead." There the middle-aged husband of Gretta Conroy finds himself unexpectedly bound to his wife's young lover, whom he regards first with jealousy and then with affection. (In the story, however, the lover is dead.) Molly is offered as a pawn not in friendship but in the father-son bond. "Betray me and be my son," Bloom half-tells Stephen. Stephen, as usual, ends by committing himself to no one, but Bloom, who has also cast off friendship, is partially at least committed to him and to Molly as father and husband. Joyce perhaps found it easier to picture this triangular relationship in *Ulysses* because he put so much of himself in both his heroes that he was at once betrayer and betrayed.

Moreover the familial relationship, while not necessarily satisfactory, is at least inevitable. In *Finnegans Wake* Joyce returns to the family situation, and the book contrasts with an early work like *Dubliners,* where most of the relationships are outside the family, or with the *Portrait,* where a break with the family is essential. It is as if, having sampled all varieties of friendship, and in *Ulysses,* fosterkinship, Joyce reverts at last to the fundamental and timeless condition of the family. Betrayal continues: in a famous passage every member of the family is revealed to have illicit relations with every other member; HCE, for example, has an incestuous interest in his daughter as strong as Bloom's interest in his son. Stanislaus Joyce remembered his brother's saying to him, "There are only two permanent things in the world, the love of a mother for her child, and the love of a man for lies." But Stanislaus thought his brother in later life had discovered still another form of love, that of a father for his daughter. In the *Portrait* the hero moved away from his father's family to friends, but every friend betrayed him; and now the hero reverts to the family, this time a family of his own making. In the family betrayal continues, yet here all the members of the family seem principally aspects of Joyce's imaginative life, alternately embracing and rejecting each other, but bound as indissolubly as the cortexes of the brain. He is the wooer and the wooed, the slayer and the slain.

The image that Joyce created of his life, and that his biographer Herbert Gorman followed him in consolidating, is heavily suffused with the character of the betrayed man, but neglects the element of desire for betrayal. No one wishes to underestimate the difficulties of writers in Ireland, which have driven so many of them to other countries. The continent of Europe is not the most miserable exchange imaginable, however. But it is characteristic of Joyce's state of mind that things never got better for him. From his talk and from Gorman's biography, one has the impression that his relations with publishers were always execrable; actually Joyce was treated extremely well by publishers from about his thirty-fourth year. In the same way, Joyce steadily represented himself as living in poverty, but as Ernest Hemingway remarked in the early 1920s, poverty found the Joyces every night at Fouquet's, where Hemingway could afford to go only once a week. Joyce forced himself into bad straits. He grew so accustomed to representing himself as a mild saint surrounded by energetic devils that Stuart Gilbert quite surprised and amused him by pointing out that he was not really in bad circumstances at all, that he was on the contrary quite lucky.

Most of the incidents in Joyce's life have to be reconsidered from this point of view. For example, in the famous quarrel in Zurich involving the English Players, Joyce represented himself as the victim of splenetic British bureaucrats. Actually, he appears to have provoked an unnecessary row quite deliberately, constructing an incident in which he would be aggrieved so he could then protest it. The humorous references to it at the end of the *Circe* episode were the artistic aftermath of his inartistic involvement. Similarly, when Mrs. McCormick abruptly withdrew her patronage from Joyce in Zurich, he fastened the blame upon a young friend of his, and Gorman says in a dark footnote which Joyce wrote for him: "Several times during Joyce's career this brusque and unexplained [change of] attitude of certain admirers of his has taken place. . . . There is no single explanation so far as these different admirers are concerned that will fit all these cases, but the fact remains that all through his life he seems to have had admiration both in its spiritual and its material form spontaneously and suddenly offered him and subsequently just as suddenly transformed into passive or open hostility." Joyce's suspicions of his young friend were altogether unfounded, but they suggest how essential it was for him to believe that his friends were, at the slightest nudge, his enemies. As in his quarrel with Nora in

1909, his anger at being victimized knew no bounds, although in both cases he was his own victim. There is a certain relish for the violent breaking of friendships; a favorite word in his early work is "sunder." No doubt in some instances Joyce had cause, but even in these he helped the betrayers along. The image in one of his later poems, of plucking his own heart out and devouring it, is a recurrent pattern in his behavior as in his works.

In actual life Joyce's urge to detach himself became itself a passion, so strong that it led him into truculence or into distrust, but, in the perverse way of art, his violent renewals of exile through the persons of his friends became a virtue. As soon as he had rejected them as friends, convinced of their propensity to betray him and of his own to be betrayed, he was free to behold them in that clear light which is one of his special contributions to fiction. His characters, except for his heroes, belong to a land which he lords as an absentee. They lack the liberating recourse of art, which enables him to recover a mastery he has dissipated in quarrels; he does not treat them with coldness, but rather with the sympathy of someone who can emerge from their nerve-racked sphere, beyond love and lies to detachment and truth. As for the heroes, particularly Bloom and Stephen, while they are not as removed as their creator from attachments, they show some of the same power to withdraw themselves. A certain insouciance and humor in Bloom prevent his taking his wife's adultery altogether to heart, and keep him also from entanglements with Martha Clifford and Gerty MacDowell. The more sombre Stephen too, when he propositions Emma Clery in *Stephen Hero,* stipulates that on the morning after their night of love they will say an eternal farewell; in the *Portrait,* when he finds a girl who symbolizes all that he desires, he makes no attempt to know her; and in *Ulysses* he withdraws also from the proffered friendship with Bloom. The heroes in most novels are drawn into situations; in Joyce's they extricate themselves from them.

Joyce told his friend Claud Sykes that, so long as he could write, he could live anywhere, in a tub, like Diogenes. Writing was itself a form of exile for him, a source of detachment. When a young man came up to him in Zurich and said, "May I kiss the hand that wrote *Ulysses?*" Joyce replied, somewhat like King Lear, "No, it did lots of other things too." Only in writing, which is also departing, is it possible to achieve the purification which comes from a continual re-baptism of the mind.

Martyr and Maze-maker

Anthony Burgess

Joyce's first attempt at forging a piece of imaginative prose out of his own artistic genesis belongs, apparently, to 1904, Bloomsyear, when the genesis was still going on. The Dublin intellectuals Eglinton and Ryan were bringing out a magazine called, after the Irish earth-goddess, *Dana*. Joyce wrote a story about himself—the renegade Catholic discovering his creative soul through sin, then striding forward to change the world—in which the technique of the Symbolists was charged with the spirit of Ibsen. Stanislaus Joyce suggested "A Portrait of the Artist" as a title; under this name it was submitted to *Dana* and promptly rejected. Still, nothing was lost. Indeed, writers are sometimes quietly relieved about rejections: they will often have second thoughts as soon as the package has slid into the post-box, seeing in their subject-matter a bigger potential than was at first apparent: many a big book has started as something for a magazine. Joyce was quick to observe that his theme deserved to be developed on the scale of a full-length novel, and so he conceived a bildungs-roman of some three hundred thousand words. Thus *Stephen Hero* was born. The writing of it seems to have proceeded, first in Dublin, then in Trieste, *pari passu* with the sketches for *Dubliners,* but Joyce was never to publish *Stephen Hero*. Most of the completed manuscript was apparently burnt—perhaps in a mood of dejection—but nearly four hundred pages survived, to be published posthumously as *Stephen Hero: Part of the first draft of "A Portrait of the Artist as a Young Man."*

From *Re Joyce*. © 1965 by Anthony Burgess. W. W. Norton, 1965.

That is how we read this long fragment—as a groping towards a masterpiece. We can see why Joyce abandoned his original scheme: it had too little shape to it, there was too much concern with recording life warm, as it was lived. The vitality of *Stephen Hero* derives mainly from its passionate egoism, the need to set down—as in a journal—everything that happens as soon as it happens, for every grain of experience is food for the greedy growing soul of the artist. Joyce always wants the whole of something. His inability to encompass, in *Stephen Hero,* the whole of a growing life, together with what that life feeds on, teaches him to be content with smaller wholes—the whole of a day in *Ulysses* and the whole of a night in *Finnegans Wake.* In every major artist there seems to be a conflict between the urge to swallow everything and the desire to select and shape. Joyce must have seen the dangers implicit in the writing of *Stephen Hero* more clearly because of his solution of the problem of *Dubliners.* It was not enough to gather a bunch of casual epiphanies and impose unity on them through the fact of mere common citizenship: Joyce arranged his stories cunningly, in a sort of genetic pattern, beginning with childhood, moving on to adolescence, adulthood, public life, and modulating to the Church through motherhood; finally, all the living and the dead, the young, the old, the frail forts they build against time and corruption, are wrapped together under the metaphysical snow. For his autobiographical novel he conceived a cognate design but was bolder in his drawing on the resources of symbolism.

The growth of the embryo and the growth of the soul mirrored each other in Joyce's personal symbolism. In the "Oxen of the Sun" episode in *Ulysses,* a history of English literature—which is a good enough record of the spiritual history of a nation—is used to symbolise embryonic growth; in *A Portrait of the Artist as a Young Man,* embryonic growth is used to symbolise the spiritual history of a young poet. There was no element of the cold and considered choice of symbols here: Joyce, as a medical student, had become fascinated by embryology; the conception and birth of his daughter Lucia pointed the mystery; his idiosyncratic passion for Nora avoided the filial but often—in his letters to her—expressed itself in the foetal. The static and passive organism, which does not move of its own volition but on which growth is miraculously imposed, is a very Joycean concept.

As soon as we meet the name of Joyce's hero we recognize that symbolism is at work, but in *Stephen Hero* that particular symbolism sticks out like a sore thumb, especially in the implausible form "Daedalus." Joyce was quick to change this to "Dedalus," which will just about stand in a naturalistic novel, but the name can only really radiate significance in a symbolic context. So the "Stephen Dedalus" of *A Portrait,* which makes naturalism serve symbolism, can sound all its harmonics—the self-elected martyrdom of literature, the wren which, in the song, is the "king of all birds" and is sacrificed on St Stephen's Day, the stones which killed a saint and which built a labyrinth, the invention of flight—flight for exile and flight for poetic creation, the image of a bird which unites the pagan name and the Christian.

A Portrait of the Artist as a Young Man has many symbols, but the fundamental one is of a creature trying to escape from the bondage of the grosser elements, earth and water, and learning painfully how to fly. The first of the five big chapters into which the book is organised begins with a child's discrete impressions—the father's fairy tale (the father comes first), the stumbling of an infant's tongue that is not yet a poet's, so that "O, the wild rose blossoms" becomes "O, the green wothe botheth," the smells of bed and father and mother, water. The embryonic soul is surrounded by a sort of amniotic fluid—urine and the sea (Stephen dances a hornpipe); as for the land, it has two colours—red and green. These are also heraldic or political colours: "Dante had two brushes in her press. The brush with the maroon velvet back was for Michael Davitt and the brush with the green velvet back was for Parnell." But the embryo is better used to darkness, and so Stephen hides under the table. Dante (Mrs Riordan, his nurse) foretells his future.

His mother said:

—O, Stephen will apologise.

Dante said:

—O, if not, the eagles will come and pull out his
eyes—
Pull out his eyes,
Apologise,
Apologise,
Pull out his eyes.

The eagle, not the wren, is still the king of all birds, but he knows who is threatening to usurp his eyrie and he counter-threatens the poet with blindness.

This opening page is a swift miracle, the sort of achievement which, in its immediacy and astonishing economy, ought to make the conventional novelist ("My first memories are of my father, a monocled hirsute man who told me stories") ashamed. Prose and subject matter have become one and inseparable; it is the first big technical breakthrough of twentieth-century prose writing and, inevitably, it looks as if anybody could have thought of it. The roots of *Ulysses* are here—to every phase of the soul its own special language; *Finnegans Wake* must seem, not a wilful aberration from sense, but a logical conclusion from that premise. If we recognise the rightness of "When you wet the bed first it is warm then it gets cold. His mother put on the oilsheet. That had the queer smell," we must accept the inevitability of "Till thousendsthee. Lps. The keys to. Given! A way a lone a last a loved a long the."

The section that follows takes Stephen to Clongowes Wood College. He is still a child, a creature of responses and not of thought, and he tries to hide from the boisterous world. The eye-pecking eagle has become a football: "The greasy leather orb flew like a heavy bird through the grey light." In the pale and chilly evening air he feels "his body small and weak amid the throng of players"; his eyes are "weak and watery." He is surrounded by mud and cold but he is also ill: a boy called Wells (appropriate name) shouldered him into the slimy water of the square ditch because he would not swop his snuffbox for a hacking chestnut. The soul is kept pushed down to its primal water and earth. Stephen hears one boy call another a "suck" and at once he hears and sees water going down a lavatory basin. The colours of earth assert themselves: "He remembered the song about the wild rose blossoms on the little green place. But you could not have a green rose. But perhaps somewhere in the world you could." A classmate, Fleming, has coloured the earth and clouds on the first page of the geography book—the earth green and the clouds maroon. We are back to Dante's brushes and—gross forces which will try to hold the emergent soul to a particular spot of earth—Irish politics. Parnell is in Stephen's mind as he shivers in the study hall:

> He wondered which was right, to be for the green or for the maroon, because Dante had ripped the green velvet back off the brush that was for Parnell one day with her scissors and had told him that Parnell was a bad man. He

wondered if they were arguing at home about that. That was called politics. There were two sides in it: Dante was on one side and his father and Mr Casey were on the other side but his mother and Uncle Charles were on no side.

When he is taken off to the school infirmary and his soul almost resigns itself to the earth ("How beautiful the words were where they said *Bury me in the old churchyard!*") he has a watery vision, full of the noise of waves, with the cry "Parnell! He is dead!" coming up from the crowd by the sea's edge. Dante, in maroon and green velvet, walks proudly and silently past.

The red of holly and the green of ivy usher in the Christmas dinner scene, with its terrible quarrel about politics and the Church and Mr Casey's heartbroken cry of "Poor Parnell! My dead king!" Stephen, old enough now to sit at table with his elders, raises a terror-stricken face to see his father's eyes full of tears. The soul is learning about the world—loyalty, treachery, the bitter divisions of faith. Other lessons come when he is back at school—the crimes of adolescence and just punishments for those crimes. But Stephen himself is punished for nothing: his glasses are broken and (the eagles are at work) he cannot see well enough to write. The prefect of studies comes into the classroom, calls Stephen a lazy little schemer and—in one of the most excruciatingly painful passages in all modern literature—beats him with a pandybat:

> A hot burning stinging tingling blow like the loud crack of a broken stick made his trembling hand crumple together like a leaf in the fire: and at the sound and the pain scalding tears were driven into his eyes. His whole body was shaking with fright, his arm was shaking and his crumpled burning livid hand shook like a loose leaf in the air. A cry sprang to his lips, a prayer to be let off. But though the tears scalded his eyes and his limbs quivered with pain and fright he held back the hot tears and the cry that scalded his throat.
> —Other hand! shouted the prefect of studies.

The peculiar objectivity of Joyce's method can be seen even in isolated words. In the paragraph that follows, Stephen draws back "his shaking arm in terror" and bursts out "into a whine of pain." "Whine" is not usually for heroes, but it is the exact word that is wanted here. Similarly, the Stephen of *Ulysses* is as capable of sneering as of picking his nose. Let traditionally unheroic connotations go hang.

And now the earthbound spirit, pandybatted to shameful lowliness, finds the courage to attempt the air. Nasty Roche tells Stephen to complain to the rector; a fellow in second of grammar says: "The senate and the Roman people declared that Dedalus had been wrongly punished." His name is a great name, like the names of great classical men in Richmal Magnall's Questions; the eagles are on his side. He complains to the rector, who gives him a kind hearing and says that it will not happen again, and walks away faster and faster towards the air. He tells his schoolfellows what he has done, and they fling their caps into the air, cheering. They hoist him up on their locked hands and carry him. He is airborne and the leitmotif is "air." But, when he is alone again, the smell of evening in the air reminds him of fields and the digging up of turnips. The sound of the cricket balls being bumped in the distance is "pick, pack, pock, puck: like drops of water in a fountain falling softly in the brimming bowl." We are back to the amniotic fluid. The foetus has had a premonition of release, but there is still a long time to go before emancipation.

In the second chapter the prose becomes staider and more periodic, suggesting the tortuous groping towards the soul's expression through school essays and reading in nineteenth-century literature. Stephen, under the old trainer Mike Flynn, is learning to run if not to fly. But words are already suggesting to him that another element awaits his fledging:

> Words which he did not understand he said over and over
> to himself till he had learnt them by heart; and through
> them he had glimpses of the real world about him. The
> hour when he too would take part in the life of that world
> seemed drawing near and in secret he began to make ready
> for the great part which he felt awaited him the nature of
> which he only dimly apprehended.

Dreams out of *The Count of Monte Cristo* nourish his pride. His first image of woman comes to him in the form of Mercedes, filling his blood with unrest. Meanwhile, the ruin of his family is under way, and he is not to go back to Clongowes. But, says his father, "there's a crack of the whip left in me yet, Stephen, old chap. We're not dead

yet, sonny. No, by the Lord Jesus (God forgive me) nor half dead."
And so the furniture caravans move the Dedalus chattels to Dublin,
and the subject matter awaits the artist. The key words are "unrest,"
"dissatisfaction," "embittered silence," "anger": the growing soul is
dragged down more than ever before by its sense of circumambient
squalor. We have the first vague glimpse of the "temptress"—the
young girl at the party, Emma Clery, who appears only in her
initials, a cipher at the head of the poem he writes for her, under
A.M.D.G. and over L.D.S.

Stephen goes to Belvedere College, so that he is still receiving a
Jesuit education. The steady thickening of the prose style matches the
"scum of disgust" that coats his palate for life; an immense amount
of detail is marked—as in the description of the Whitsuntide play in
which Stephen performs—but there is no emergence of any single
image. The sheer multiplicity of daily life bewilders the soul, and the
tortures of pubescence additionally hold back flight. But one bird,
his schoolfriend Heron, has achieved one kind of emancipation—the
giggling world of bazaars and tennis parties and cigarettes. Heron
taunts Stephen with Emma's interest in him ("And what part does
Stephen take, Mr Dedalus? And will Stephen not sing, Mr
Dedalus?") and, threatening playfully to strike him with his cane,
tries to make Stephen admit that he is a sly dog. This easy world of
banter and flirtation is one the young poet cannot enter. Heron is
superficial, philistine Ireland with little, though painful, claws. It was
Heron, Stephen remembers, who, over a year ago, had tried to make
him admit that Byron was no good—a bad man and an atheist, hence
(in Irish logic) a poor poet. Then Stephen had not given in and he had
been beaten with a cabbage stump as well as a cane; it was the
beginning of his literary martyrdom. Now he glibly recites the
Confiteor to the indulgent laughter of Heron and his friend Wallis. He
cannot really hold anger or resentment for very long; like peel from
a fruit, all strong emotion becomes swiftly and smoothly detached
from him. He is preparing for the single commitment of art.
Meanwhile, he has to act the part of an aged pedant in the school
play. The curtain falls and, in a complex and intolerable seizure of
emotions he cannot understand—pride (wounded), hope (fallen),
desire (baffled)—he runs and runs, as once before down the corridor
leading from the rector's study at Clongowes. But this time it is
down a hill—"at breakneck speed." At the bottom of the hill the
smell of horse piss and rotted straw calms his heart. He must prepare

for a greater descent into further squalor. He is still not ready for take-off.

Stephen goes with his father to Cork, Simon Dedalus's old city. Some vague business connected with saving the family itself from a too precipitous descent takes them there. Stephen's pubescent torments find images of shame. In the Queen's College, where Mr Dedalus was once a medical student, he meets the word "Foetus" cut several times on a desk. "The sudden legend startled his blood." Unbidden and derived from no known memory, a vision of the act of inscription springs up before him:

> A broadshouldered student with a moustache was cutting in the letters with a jack knife, seriously. Other students stood or sat near him laughing at his handiwork. One jogged his elbow. The big student turned on him, frowning. He was dressed in loose grey clothes and had tan boots.

Stephen is to know other, seemingly pointless, epiphanies of this order. The present visionary shock frames a significant word. He is still held down in the womb of matter, longing for birth but compelled to remain an embryo driven by an enclosing will to take further, more grotesque, shapes before release into the air. He recognises his formlessness, the sleep of pre-birth which is represented to him as death. "His childhood was dead or lost and with it his soul capable of simple joys and he was drifting amid life like the barren shell of the moon."

The shell is a specious one. The outer life of Stephen is one of academic success, and he even wins thirty-three pounds as an exhibition and essay prize. With the money he tries "to build a breakwater of order and elegance against the sordid tide of life without him and to dam up, by rules of conduct and active interests and new filial relations, the powerful recurrence of the tide within him." But he fails, recognises that he must succumb to sin, and lets the tide break. In the brothel district of Dublin he finds what he must have.

Can the soul descend any lower? The world that Joyce now describes is one of dull light, through which the soul thuds and blunders, taking a kind of crass pleasure in its own degradation. Sin follows sin, fumblings with whores are matched by a gross appetite for greasy mutton stews. Matter has reasserted itself, but the clogged soul has no desire to be free. Yet one exalted image prevails, though hopelessly: Mercedes has appropriately changed to the Blessed Virgin, an allomorph of the *Ewig-weibliche,* the eternal woman.

> If ever his soul, reentering her dwelling shyly after the frenzy of his body's lust had spent itself, was turned towards her whose emblem is the morning star, "bright and musical, telling of heaven and infusing peace," it was when her names were murmured softly by lips whereon there still lingered foul and shameful words, the savour itself of a lewd kiss.

As for the lips of the embryo artist himself, they seem to have forfeited the right of golden utterance. At the beginning of the book they stuttered ("O, the green wothe botheth"); now they have yielded to a pressure "darker than the swoon of sin." They cannot receive the Eucharist, not yet.

The soul can, of course, descend lower, for it can descend to the Pit. Now follows the incredible and most unjesuitical retreat, in which Father Arnall's sermons on hell are presented unedited, the utter limit of naturalism. Here is the final victory of natural elements which have taken on divine intensity and duration. There is no air now, only stench and corruption and fire. Stephen's terror is so great that it breeds hallucinations: faces watch and voices murmur:

> —We knew perfectly well of course that although it was bound to come to the light he would find considerable difficulty in endeavouring to try to induce himself to try to endeavour to ascertain the spiritual plenipotentiary and so we knew of course perfectly well—

The verbal technique moves closer to *Ulysses.* The image of personal hell is almost a stage direction out of the brothel scene:

> A field of stiff weeds and thistles and tufted nettlebunches. Thick among the tufts of rank stiff growth lay battered canisters and clots and coils of solid excrement. A faint marsh light struggling upwards from all the ordure through the bristling greygreen weeds. An evil smell, faint and foul as the light, curled upwards sluggishly out of the canisters and from the stale crusted dung.

The field is full of grey satyrs. The horror of the vision is intensified by the trivial sordidness of some of the properties—the canisters, stale excrement, a torn flannel waistcoat round the ribs of one of the creatures. It is authentic hell. Stephen cries for air.

He is not the only one. I still find it difficult to read the hell chapter without some of the sense of suffocation I felt when I first met it, at the age of fifteen, myself a Catholic looking for emancipation. I was hurled back into conformity by this very sermon and this very vision. As for Stephen, he runs blindly to confession and, in a white dream of holiness recaptured, receives the Eucharist. Everything is white—pudding, eggs, flowers, the altar cloth, the wafer, Stephen's soul. The lips that kissed a whore at the end of the preceding chapter now open for the reception of Christ. But, by a fine irony, the elevation that the soul has awaited belongs to a different order of reality from what religion represents. Stephen's long penance, with its curious mortifications of the flesh, seems to bear no real spiritual fruit. He finds himself in bondage to a quantitative concept of salvation which expresses itself in very materialistic terms:

> He seemed to feel his soul in devotion pressing like fingers
> the keyboard of a great cash register and to see the amount
> of his purchase start forth immediately in heaven, not as a
> number but as a frail column of incense or as a slender
> flower.

He is still waiting for the real ciborium, and—the irony maintained—he senses its coming when his spiritual director asks him whether he has ever felt that he had a vocation. He nearly says yes, but he withholds the word. The priest means something very specific. "The Reverend Stephen Dedalus, S.J." Stephen is aware of temptation, but the vision of himself as a priest is at once confused with the images of the soul's repression we have already met in the Clongowes episodes. "His lungs dilated and sank as if he were inhaling a warm moist unsustaining air, and he smelt again the moist warm air which hung in the bath in Clongowes above the sluggish turfcoloured water."

Stephen at last knows that literature is his vocation, priestly enough since its function is the transmutation of lowly accidents to godly essence. Through art he can come to terms with the down-dragging stuff of material life:

The faint sour stink of rotted cabbages came towards him from the kitchen gardens on the rising ground above the river. He smiled to think that it was this disorder, the misrule and confusion of his father's house and the stagnation of vegetable life, which was to win the day in his soul.

He walks towards the sea and observes the raw white bodies of his old schoolfellows, foetuses that will never emerge to outer life, flopping about in the water. But they at least recognise, even in joke, the "mild proud sovereignty" of the poet, and his name, which they call, "seemed to him a prophecy"—"Stephanos Dedalos! Bous Stephanoumenos! Bous Stephaneforos!" And now, for the first time, Stephen sees a winged form over the waves, slowly mounting the sky. It is Daedalus, the fabulous artificer. The soul at last takes wing:

> His heart trembled in an ecstasy of fear and his soul was in flight. His soul was soaring in an air beyond the world and the body he knew was purified in a breath and delivered of incertitude and made radiant and commingled with the element of the spirit. An ecstasy of flight made radiant his eyes and wild his breath and tremulous and wild and radiant his windswept limbs.

He wants to cry out his sense of deliverance, in the voice of a hawk or eagle. Fire, which had been presented to him as a property of hell, is part of the air-world: his blood and body burn for adventure. All that is now needed to mediate between earth and heaven is some angelic vision of a woman who is neither a whore nor the Virgin Mary. Stephen sees a girl standing in a rivulet, "alone and still, gazing out to sea." No word passes between them, but her image enters his soul forever. She embodies the call of life. He falls asleep in rapture on the earth, and the earth takes him to her breast. The grosser elements no longer drag him down: they have become sanctified by his newly found power of flight. The earth is for wandering and the sea for travel. He is master of the four elements. And then we remember the inscription on the flyleaf of the young Stephen's geography, back in Clongowes:

> Stephen Dedalus
> Class of Elements
> Clongowes Wood College

Sallins
County Kildare
Ireland
Europe
The World
The Universe.

It is, we see, a manifesto of conquest, and now it is beginning to be fulfilled.

Stephen Dedalus and Women: A Portrait of the Artist as a Young Misogynist

Suzette Henke

MOTHER AND CHILD

Female characters are present everywhere and nowhere in *A Portrait of the Artist as a Young Man*. They pervade the novel, yet remain elusive. Their sensuous figures haunt the developing consciousness of Stephen Dedalus and provide a foil against which he defines himself as both man and artist. Like everything in *A Portrait,* women are portrayed almost exclusively from Stephen's point of view. Seen through his eyes and colored by his fantasies, they often appear as one-dimensional projections of a narcissistic imagination. Females emerge as the psychological "other," forceful antagonists in the novel's dialectical structure. They stand as emblems of the flesh—frightening reminders of sex, generation, and death.

At the dawn of infantile consciousness, Stephen perceives the external world in terms of complementary pairs: male and female, father and mother, politics and religion, Davitt and Parnell. Baby Tuckoo's cosmos is organized in binary structures that set the stage for a dialectic of personal development. From a psychological perspective, the mother seems to be in touch with the overwhelming chaos of nature. The father, in contrast, offers a model of logocentric control.

Stephen sees his father as masculine and aloof, visually separated by a glass monocle and a hairy face. The male parent is bearer of the

From *Women and Joyce,* edited by Suzette Henke and Elaine Unkeless. © 1982 by the Board of Trustees of the University of Illinois. University of Illinois Press, 1982.

word; he tells a story that appeals to the child's imagination and awakens him to a sense of individual identity. The female parent relates to the boy primarily as caretaker; she satisfies her son's physical desires and encourages his artistic expression by playing the piano. This sweet-smelling guardian is closely associated with sensuous comfort and bodily joy:

> When you wet the bed first it is warm then it gets cold. His mother put on the oilsheet. That had the queer smell.
>
> His mother had a nicer smell than his father. She played on the piano the sailor's hornpipe for him to dance. He danced.

At the outset of *A Portrait,* Stephen perceives his mother as a powerful and beneficent source of physical pleasure. She ministers to each of the five senses. It is the "nice" mother, however, who is one of the women principally responsible for introducing Stephen to a hostile external world and to the laws of social conformity. The first of the many imperatives that thwart the boy's ego, "apologise," is associated with matriarchal threats:

> He hid under the table. His mother said:
> —O, Stephen will apologise.
> Dante said:
> —O, if not, the eagles will come and pull out his eyes.

Dante and Mrs. Dedalus both represent the inhibitions of a reality principle that begins, at this point, to take precedence over the gratifications of infantile narcissism. They mutually demand the repression of libidinous tendencies and a conquest of the id in favor of a developing social ego. As Dorothy Dinnerstein explains in *The Mermaid and the Minotaur,* it is usually a woman who serves as "every infant's first love, first witness and first boss. . . . The initial experience of dependence on a largely uncontrollable outside source of good is focused on a woman, and so is the earliest experience of vulnerability to disappointment and pain."

According to Freudian theory, the primordial conflict between male and female takes root in the infant's early discovery of a world alien to his sensibilities and antagonistic to the demands of his omnipotent will. As the child begins to distinguish between ego and environment, between self and other, he becomes aware of a dangerous threat to his own struggle for individuation. In a process of psychological transference, he symbolically equates the mother or a mother-surrogate with the enemy that frustrates his desires and threatens to engulf his newly acquired sense of self. The female takes on extraordinary and mysterious powers. A goddess in her authority, she is unconsciously identified with the hated flesh that eludes the infant's control.

As Simone de Beauvoir explains in *The Second Sex,* the male child associates his mother, and consequently his image of the female, with the viscosity and "immanence" of physical existence. He develops a conviction that women are bound by the generative demands of the species, and the presence of his mother becomes an ominous reminder of the shame of his animal nature and the reality of personal extinction. "The uncleanness of birth is reflected upon the mother. . . . And if the little boy remains in early childhood sensually attached to the maternal flesh, when he grows older, becomes socialized, and takes note of his individual existence, this same flesh frightens him . . . calls him back to those realms of immanence whence he would fly."

"Reproduction is the beginning of death." So argued Hegel, and so argues Stephen's friend Temple. The Manichean dichotomy between flesh and spirit, body and mind, has long been allied in the writings of male philosophers with the basic polarity between the sexes. Stephen vies with Nietzsche and with Schopenhauer when, in *Stephen Hero,* he proposes a misogynist "theory of dualism which would symbolise the twin eternities of spirit and nature in the twin eternities of male and female." According to Simone de Beauvoir, man's symbolic association of woman with the flesh reflects a disdain for human corporality. The male identifies himself as "spirit" by virtue of his own subjective consciousness; he then perceives the female as "the Other, who limits and denies him."

The antagonism of these "twin eternities" is impressed on Stephen at an early age. He disdains his mother's feminine vulnerability and thinks that she is "not nice" when she cries. Like most young boys, Stephen begins to interpret his relationship with his mother as an obstacle to more grown-up ties with his own sex. Armed with ten shillings and his father's injunctions toward a code of masculine loyalty, he "manfully" enters the competitive joust of life at Clongowes. He determines to adopt an ethic of male stoicism because "his father had told him . . . whatever he did, never to peach on a fellow."

In a world of social Darwinism, Stephen defines himself as both literally and figuratively marginal. Caught in a stampede of "flashing eyes and muddy boots," he is horrified by the bestial fury of the crowd—"fellows . . . struggling and groaning . . . and stamping." The boy mentally takes refuge in artistic evocations of the family hearth, protected by beneficent female spirits—Mother, Dante, and the servant Brigid. As he relives the horror of being shouldered into a urinal ditch by the bully Wells, Stephen projects himself beyond the rats and the scum to an apparently dissociated reverie. He recalls his mother sitting by the fire in hot "jewelly slippers" that exude a "lovely warm smell." Alienated from a brutal male environment, Stephen longs to return to his mother. In true Oedipal fashion, he focuses on the fetishistic symbols of her warm feet, sexual totems that offer both kinesthetic and olfactory satisfaction in compensation for the stench and the slimy touch of the chilling water.

Incarcerated in the infirmary, Stephen hallucinates his own death and burial. He also reverts to infant attachment and imagines writing a letter begging his mother to "come and take me home." "He longed to be at home and lay his head on his mother's lap." But he distinguishes between this maternal sanctuary and "his father's house," "cold and dark under the seawall."

In a confused way, Stephen tries to fathom the mysteries of Oedipal attraction. He is unable to differentiate between filial and erotic love and feels perplexed when Wells unites the two in a sexual conundrum: "Tell us, Dedalus, do you kiss your mother before you go to bed?" Stephen desires the soft wetness of his mother's lips, but is baffled by the moral implications of a riddle that would challenge the saintliness of Aloysius Gonzaga. Later, in chapter 5, when Cranly asks Stephen whether he "loves his mother," the young man is still unable to respond. "I don't know what your words mean," he replies.

As the curious child stumbles toward manhood, he feels compelled to cast off allegiance to maternal figures. His childhood educator Dante, "a clever woman and a wellread woman" who teaches him geography and lunar lore, is supplanted by male instructors: "Father Arnall knew more than Dante because he was a priest." The Jesuit masters invite Stephen to ponder the mysteries of religion, death, canker, and cancer. They introduce him to a system of male authority and discipline, to a pedagogical regimen that will insure his "correct training" and proper socialization. Through examinations that pit red rose against white, Yorks against Lancastrians, they make education an aggressive game of simulated warfare. The students, like soldiers, are depersonalized through institutional surveillance.

At home for Christmas dinner, Stephen assimilates the knowledge that rabid women like Dante Riordan support ecclesiastical authority in the name of moral righteousness. Like the "sow that eats her farrow," Dante is willing to sacrifice Parnell as a political scapegoat. In the face of Mr. Casey's Fenianism and Simon's contemptuous snorting, she declares the Catholic clergy "the apple of God's eye." Like a perverted Eve, Dante defends the ecclesiastical apple against Ireland's republican leader, that "devil out of hell" crushed by an irate populace. She suggests a formidable alliance between the Catholic church and bourgeois respectability.

In the battle between male and female, Mother Church emerges as a bastion of sexual repression defended by hysterical women. Dante's own credibility is negated by spinsterhood and involuntary celibacy. Stephen "had heard his father say that she was a spoiled nun and that she had come out of the convent in the Alleghanies when her brother had got the money from the savages for the trinkets and the chainies." Stephen's male role models, Simon Dedalus and John Casey, assert masculine prowess through acts of republican fervor. Hence Casey's braggadocio in recounting his triumph over the hag who screamed "whore": "I had my mouth full of tobacco juice. I bent down to her and *Phth!* says I to her like that . . . right into her eye." In this tale of heroism, Casey conquers the malevolent crone— the folkloric witch, hag, or "mother-in-law" who caricatures female dementia. Spitting in her eye, he symbolically achieves a talismanic victory through sexual violation of the phallic mother. Casey expects women to function as docile bodies—peacemakers like Mary Dedalus and mollifying agents of social arbitration.

When Stephen again returns to Clongowes, he realizes that his mother cannot offer a viable sanctuary from the male-dominated power structure that controls the outer world. He must learn to survive in a society that protects bullies like Wells and sadists like Father Dolan, that condones brutality, and that takes advantage of the weak and the helpless. The pandybat incident at the end of chapter 1 symbolically reinforces the rites of objectification characteristic of Jesuit training. Father Dolan's authority is absolute and unquestioned. He relies on patriarchal privilege and assumes a "panoptical" vision: "Father Dolan will be in to see you every day."

Branded as a "lazy little schemer," Stephen must endure the ignominy of being misnamed and robbed of subjective identity.

The young boy is being socialized into what Philip Slater identifies as a culture of male narcissism. According to Slater, single-sex education and the separation of male children from the emotional refuge of the family promotes misogyny, narcissism, and a terror of the female. Boy children suffer from an "unconscious fear of being feminine, which leads to 'protest masculinity,' exaggeration of the difference between men and women" (*The Glory of Hera*). Once the child is deprived of maternal affection, he "seeks compensation through self-aggrandizement—renouncing love for admiration—and in this he is encouraged by the achievement pressure placed upon him, and presumably by the myriad narcissistic role models he finds around him. He becomes vain, hypersensitive, invidious, ambitious, . . . boastful, and exhibitionistic."

Stephen's appeal to Father Conmee is motivated not only by optimistic faith in a male-controlled world, but by personal vanity and a tendency toward exhibitionism. His youthful vision is blurred, idealistic, and Panglossian. He naively believes that he will be exonerated simply by presenting his case before a higher patriarch. In his confrontation with the rector, Stephen makes a symbolic rite of passage through the primordial chambers of racial and ecclesiastical history. He asserts his budding manhood against totalitarian power and is acclaimed a revolutionary hero by "the Senate and the Roman people." But the triumphant child later discovers the aftermath of his rebellion: Dolan and Conmee, in smug condescension, "had a famous laugh together over it." Stephen has unwittingly played the ingenuous fool at the court of his Jesuit masters. In a bold attempt to assert masculine independence, he has served merely as an object of paternal amusement.

VIRGIN AND WHORE

In chapter 5 of *A Portrait,* Cranly asks Stephen if he would deflower a virgin. His companion replies by posing another question: "Is that not the ambition of most young gentlemen?" Figuratively, it is Stephen's ambition throughout the novel to "deflower" the Blessed Virgin of Catholicism. He wants to supplant the Catholic Madonna with a profane surrogate, an aesthetic muse rooted in sensuous reality.

In chapter 2, Stephen vainly searches for the romantic figure of a woman who will mediate his artistic transfiguration. Identifying with the Count of Monte Cristo, he conjures up adolescent fantasies of a beautiful Mercedes, whom he stalks in the suburbs of Blackrock. He longs "to meet in the real world the unsubstantial image which his soul so constantly beheld. . . . They would meet quietly as if they had known each other and had made their tryst. . . . He would fade into something impalpable under her eyes and then in a moment, he would be transfigured. Weakness and timidity and inexperience would fall from him in that magic moment." It is essential that the figure of Mercedes be "unsubstantial" and free of physical dross. She must obliterate any palpable connection with the corporeal prison of the body. The semi-religious scene suggests beatific transformation in the darkness and silence of a moonlit garden. The romantic heroine, however, releasing her lover from the shackles of youthful inexperience, blesses him with nothing less than the power of refusal. In spiritualizing his life, she paradoxically endows him with sufficient grace to transcend the demands of sexual love.

When Stephen dreams of himself as Edmond Dantes, he identifies with a man betrayed by his friends and his mistress, unjustly exiled and imprisoned, but eventually able to wreak revenge on those who failed him. Monte Cristo's adventures culminate in a "sadly proud gesture of refusal": "Madam, I never eat muscatel grapes." Mercedes is an "untouchable" mistress, tainted by collaboration with her lover's enemies. Stephen admires the self-sufficiency of Dantes, the isolated hero who conquers the woman he loves by rejecting his amorous need for her body.

Art promises to invest Stephen with the powers of priest and shaman—the ability to confront the mysteries of creation while tasting the "joy of loneliness." Before the tantalizing face of Emma, "cowled" in nun's veiling, Stephen forces himself to remain calm and controlled, "a tranquil watcher of the scene before him." "He saw her urge her vanities, her fine dress and sash and long black stockings, and knew that he had yielded to them a thousand times. Yet a voice within him spoke above the noise of his dancing heart, asking him would he take her gift to which he had only to stretch out his hand." In Stephen's imagination, Emma becomes a nubile temptress—Mercedes in Dublin garb, Eve in nun's habit. He interprets her gestures as "flattering, taunting, searching, exciting his heart" and speculates: "She too wants me to catch hold of her . . . and kiss her."

To the reader, the adolescent Emma is hardly a Circean figure. She seems shy and coy, gaily flirtatious and mildly seductive. "She came up to his step many times and went down to hers again between their phrases and once or twice stood close beside him for some moments." Like Stephen, Emma probably feels confused by the excitations of a budding sexuality. Her gestures of affection are limited to the subtle patterns of courtship available in nineteenth-century Ireland to a young girl who wants to attract a suitor but to remain pure, chaste, and respectable.

Like the Count of Monte Cristo, Stephen turns away from Emma in proud abnegation. He will possess his mistress wholly through art. In Byronic verses written to E———— C————, "the kiss, which had been withheld by one, was given by both." Poetry offers aesthetic compensation for frustrated erotic desire. The stirrings of adolescent sexuality are deftly sublimated through lyrical fulfillment beneath the "balmy breeze and the maiden lustre of the moon." The artist's mind is cold, chaste, and detached, like that of the virginal muse Diana. His disciplined verses statically embalm the moment of romantic epiphany. Emotional mutuality has been restricted to art: Stephen feels fulfilled, but Emma is left to pine in her nun-like shroud. Her desires are safely crystallized in Byronic verses framed by two Jesuit mottoes.

The night of the Whitsuntide play, Stephen remembers the touch of Emma's hand and the sight of dark eyes that "invited and unnerved him." When Emma eludes him after the play, he feels the pang of "wounded pride and fallen hope and baffled desire." Dashing to an alley behind the Dublin morgue, he soberly takes comfort in the "good odour" of "horse piss and rotted straw." The enigmatic scene psychologically gives vent to Stephen's terror of the female. As the source of physical generation, woman serves as a reminder of animality, bodily decomposition, excrement, and death. Stephen's sentiment is Thomistic and medieval, reminiscent of religious triptychs that portray a woman first at the height of beauty, then aged and wrinkled, and finally as a skeleton bedecked in morbid finery. Stephen mentally projects onto Emma images of decay and corruption. He is accosted by his carnal connection with the world; and, like the medieval fathers of the church, he tries to rebel against mortality by renouncing the fires of lust. As Saint Augustine wryly noted, "We are born between feces and urine" [*Inter faeces et urinam nascimur*]. Joyce's young artist is well on his way to developing a similar excremental vision of sex. Birth and death are so closely linked to physical nature that they are easily allied in the misogynist mind. Rotting bodies in the morgue and rotting straw convince Stephen that "reproduction is the beginning of death."

Simon Dedalus nostalgically believes that *"Tis youth and folly / Makes young men marry."* Stephen, freed of his father's notions about youth and innocence, confines his erotic activities to "monstrous" reveries, wild orgies of the imagination in which the female is reduced to a powerless object of male fantasy. Stephen is horrified at seeing the word "Foetus" scrawled on a desk, perhaps because it suggests frustrated sexuality and the souls "impossibilised" by his onanistic rites; or perhaps because it links him with the rude, lascivious males of his father's generation. "Nothing stirred within his soul but a cold cruel and loveless lust." "He wanted to sin with another of his kind, to force another being to sin with him and to exult with her in sin."

The image of Mercedes traverses the background of Stephen's memory, but the transfiguration he once sought is consummated in the embrace of a Dublin whore. Stephen is no longer the Count of Monte Cristo when the "holy encounter" occurs. The sexual imagery at the end of chapter 2 is ironically inverted. As Stephen feels the shadow of a streetwalker "moving irresistibly upon him," he figuratively suffers the "agony of its penetration" and surrenders to a "murmurous . . . flood" of physical desire. The fusion of erotic and romantic imagery degenerates into a vague ritual of sexual initiation, celebrated before a phantasmal altar illumined by "yellow gasflames." Traditional symbols are reversed, and Stephen envisions himself in the role of sacrificial virgin, raped by a phallic figure and flooded with seminal streams. His "cry for an iniquitous abandonment" again evokes an excremental vision of sex. The sound is "but the echo of an obscene scrawl which he had read on the oozing wall of a urinal."

When Stephen yields to the prostitute's solicitations, he resembles a child about to "burst into hysterical weeping." The perfumed female recalls his "nice-smelling" mother. Clothed in a long pink gown, she leads him into a womb-like chamber, "warm and lightsome." Her round arms offer a maternal caress. Soothed like a baby by the "warm calm rise and fall of her breast," Stephen momentarily retrieves the illusion of infant satiety: "He wanted to be held firmly in her arms, to be caressed slowly, slowly, slowly. In her arms he felt that he had suddenly become strong and fearless and sure of himself. But his lips would not bend to kiss her. . . . He closed his eyes, surrendering himself to her, body and mind, conscious of nothing in the world but the dark pressure of her softly parting lips."

Stephen feels, at last, transfigured by a woman. "He was in another world; he had awakened from a slumber of centuries." His vision of the female, however, has remained essentially unchanged. The traditional dichotomy between virgin and whore, madonna and temptress, breaks down in the young man's imagination. For him, all women encompass both roles. As a child, he feared the sexual implications of his mother's kiss. He proudly spurns the romantic Mercedes and finds temporary salvation in the arms of a prostitute, who exacts the kiss earlier withheld from Emma. All the women in Stephen's life are both nurturant and demanding. They are sporadically aloof, solicitous, and sexually receptive. Emma tempted Stephen and fled—only to be transformed into a lyrical muse, then to be rejected in a cathartic scene of ascetic renunciation. The whore is an ambivalent figure of masculine aggression and feminine protection. She demands erotic surrender, yet shelters her adolescent charge in a tender, maternal embrace.

The Catholic Virgin

Like Sartre's hell in *Huis Clos,* the notion of damnation that Stephen gleans from the priest's retreat sermon involves other people—bodies crowded together after death in noisome, rotting putrefaction. "All the filth of the world, all the offal and scum of the world, we are told, shall run there as to a vast and reeking sewer. . . . And then imagine this sickening stench, multiplied a millionfold, . . . a huge and rotting human fungus."

As the "jeweleyed harlots" of Stephen's sins dance before his fevered imagination, the boy is horrified that he has besmirched the sacred figure of Emma by making her the object of his masturbatory fantasies: "The image of Emma appeared before him and, under her eyes, the flood of shame rushed forth anew from his heart. If she knew to what his mind had subjected her or how his brutelike lust had torn and trampled upon her innocence! Was that boyish love? Was that chivalry? Was that poetry?" At the same time, Stephen believes that Emma has "erred" by serving as erotic stimulus for his nightly orgies.

He feels that he has violated both Emma's honor and his own code of chivalry—not to mention the rigorous ethic of purity enforced by Irish Catholicism. Emma, he decides, shall serve as his envoy to the Blessed Mother. He imagines a scene of heavenly confrontation with the Catholic Virgin, who enjoins them to "take hands. . . . You have erred but you are always my children." With the help of Emma, Stephen plans to recoup his spiritual losses. He and his beloved, under the aegis of the Virgin Mary, will embark on a journey toward forgiveness and salvation.

Without the innocent and virginal Emma, Stephen is as "helpless and hopeless" as the souls of the damned. He hallucinates a vision of the libidinous inferno prepared especially for him: "That was his hell. God had allowed him to see the hell reserved for his sins: stinking, bestial, malignant, a hell of lecherous goatish fiends. For him! For him!"

To escape the threat of damnation, Stephen must be willing to purge himself of erotic desire. He must triumph over carnal concupiscence by refusing the impure thoughts that stimulate erection. Terrified not only of woman, but of the body and its sexual needs, Stephen is moved simultaneously to renounce Satan, the female, and his own genitalia. Catholicism demands that he psychologically castrate himself by consenting to a guilty dissociation of ego and id. He cannot identify with the antagonistic penis that seems to operate with a will of its own: "Was that then he or an inhuman thing moved by a lower soul than his soul? His soul sickened at the thought of a torpid snaky life feeding itself out of the tender marrow of his life and fattening upon the slime of lust." Haunted by grotesque fantasies of sexual alienation, Stephen feels "possessed by a magic not of himself. . . . That organ by which he thought to assert himself does not obey him; heavy with unsatisfied desires, unexpectedly becoming erect, . . . it manifests a suspicious and capricious vitality" (*The Second Sex*).

In order to confess his sins of impurity, Stephen must revert to a state of childhood innocence. He allows himself to be infantilized, "for God loved little children and suffered them to come to Him. It was a terrible and a sad thing to sin. But God was merciful to poor sinners who were truly sorry." Stephen resolves to amend his life for the sake of "atonement" with the Christian community and reintegration into a state of grace and beatitude: "He would be at one with others and with God. He would love his neighbor. He would love God Who had made and loved him. He would kneel and pray with others and be happy."

Stephen determines to repress the emergence of adolescent sexuality and to repent of the one sin that mortifies him even more than murder. The female temptress has reduced his soul to a syphilitic chancre, "festering and oozing like a sore, a squalid stream of vice." Repelled by the lurid imagery of venereal disease, Stephen humbles himself before the "old and weary voice" of his father-priest-confessor. The church's medicine man will cure his wound, rescue him from the siren, and offer a "life of grace and virtue and happiness." The priest invokes the Blessed Virgin Mary as spiritual guardian of Christian "manliness." Chanting simple declarative sentences that echo catechetical instruction, he exhorts his charge to renounce the sins of the flesh, especially masturbation: "It is a terrible sin. It kills the body and it kills the soul. It is the cause of many crimes and misfortunes. Give it up, my child, for God's sake. It is dishonorable and unmanly. . . . Pray to our mother Mary to help you. She will help you, my child. Pray to Our Blessed Lady when that sin comes into your mind."

In his repentance, Stephen turns back to the woman emblematic of Catholic worship. As prefect of Our Blessed Lady's Sodality, he will cling to purity, spiritualize his life, and engage in prolific acts of piety. With the help of the Virgin Mary, Stephen will sublimate his sexual needs and attempt to recapture the prepubescent calm characteristic of juvenile innocence.

The Bird-Girl: Aesthetic Muse

In his return to ritualistic devotion, Stephen has actually become involved in an aesthetic love affair with his own soul. The anima, the feminine aspect of the psyche, has won his passion and holds him enthralled. Like Narcissus, Stephen has fallen in love with his projected self-image clothed in female garb. "The attitude of rapture in sacred art, the raised and parted hands, the parted lips and eyes as of one about to swoon, became for him an image of the soul in prayer, humiliated and faint before her Creator." In the glorified female, "man also perceives his mysterious double; man's soul is Psyche, a woman" (*The Second Sex*). The feminine side of Stephen's identity, personified as the soul, swoons in erotic ecstasy before her creator, as the young man once swooned in the arms of a prostitute.

The Catholic priesthood offers Stephen a chance to consummate this narcissistic love affair with his psyche. It bequeaths on the soul the magical power of transubstantiation. And it promises a rite of passage into male mysteries that successfully counteract female authority: "No angel or archangel in heaven, no saint, not even the Blessed Virgin herself has the power of a priest of God." A Jesuit vocation would guarantee Stephen ascendancy over the Catholic matriarch. By virtue of the "secret knowledge and secret power" of an exclusively masculine fraternity, he would be admitted to the inner sanctum of male religious privilege.

But the price of this "awful power of which angels and saints stood in reverence" is the "grave and ordered and passionless life" of Jesuit conformity. Stephen is convinced that his destiny is to be unique and isolated, "elusive of social or religious orders." And so he chooses "the misrule and confusion of his father's house" over the pomp and ceremony of religious ritual. He will commit himself to the pagan priesthood of Father Daedalus, "the fabulous artificer, . . . a symbol of the artist forging anew in his workshop out of the sluggish matter of the earth a new soaring impalpable imperishable being."

Stephen's artistic vocation seems to be confirmed by an encounter with a woman who evokes a luminous vision of earthly beauty: "A girl stood before him in midstream, alone and still, gazing out to sea. She seemed like one whom magic had changed into the likeness of a strange and beautiful seabird. Her long slender bare legs were delicate as a crane's and pure save where an emerald trail of seaweed had fashioned itself as a sign upon the flesh. Her thighs, fuller and soft-hued as ivory, were bared almost to the hips where the white fringes of her drawers were like featherings of soft white down."

The woman revealed in Stephen's epiphany amalgamates the images of pagan and Christian iconography. She is both mortal and angelic, sensuous and serene. Her soft-hued, ivory thighs recall Eileen's ivory hands and the figure of the Catholic Virgin, Tower of Ivory. Her avian transformation harks back to the Greek myth of Leda and the swan. And her bosom, like "the breast of some darkplumaged dove," suggests the Holy Ghost, traditionally represented as a dove in Christian art. Stephen, as purveyor of the Word, imaginatively begets a surrogate Holy Spirit in his ecstatic vision of the bird-girl.

At this point in the novel, Joyce's ironic gaze is subtle but implicit. If Stephen feels sexual arousal in the presence of the exposed girl, he quickly sublimates erotic agitation beneath effusions of purple prose. The young man catches sight of an attractive woman and immediately detaches himself from participation in the scene. His reaction is static, purged of desire or loathing. Aesthetic fantasy quenches any impulse to approach the girl, to reach out and touch her, or to establish physical contact. Stephen must distance and "depersonalize" the tempting figure by making her into a species of aesthetic prey.

As the young woman rises out of the sea, she is reminiscent of Venus, the goddess of love born of the ocean foam. She is pure and virginal, yet "an emerald trail of seaweed" functions as a sign of mortality stamped on her flesh. She belongs to the mundane world of decay and corruption, and the vegetation clinging to her flesh suggests a viscous image of entrapment. The woman appears as an "angel of mortal youth and beauty, an envoy from the fair courts of life." It is significant that Joyce, in his 1904 essay "A Portrait of the Artist," uses similar phrases to describe a phantasmal image evoked by the Dublin red light district: "Beneficent one! . . . thou camest timely, as a witch to the agony of self devourer, an envoy from the fair courts of life."

Like an Irish Circe, the nymph in *A Portrait* has the potential to drag Stephen down into the emerald-green nets of Dublin paralysis. As a realistic figure, the wading girl implicitly threatens Stephen with the institutional bondage of courtship and marriage associated with physical attraction. The young man knows that he may look but not touch, admire but not speak. He glorifies the woman as an angelic messenger from the "fair courts of life," but he never considers joining her in the teeming ocean waters.

Afraid of the "waters circumfluent in space" that symbolize female fluidity, Stephen is determined to control the world of physiological process by "freezing" life in the stasis of art. His "spiritual-heroic refrigerating apparatus" has already begun to implement this flight from woman. As an artist, Stephen can capture and crystallize the "eternal feminine" in the sacramental but icy realm of aesthetic consciousness. "Her image had passed into his soul for ever and no word had broken the holy silence of his ecstasy."

At nightfall, Stephen feels his soul "swooning into some new world, fantastic, dim, uncertain as under sea, traversed by cloudy shapes and beings. A world, a glimmer, or a flower?" His spirit seems to embark on an archetypal journey through Hades to the multifoliate rose of Dante's beatific vision. The bird-girl has served as Stephen's profane virgin, a Beatrice who ushers him into the circle of heavenly experience. The Dantesque underworld may, in fact, symbolize the artistic unconscious. And the pre-Raphaelite rose imagery, popular with the early Yeats and with the Rhymers of the nineties, surely casts a satirical light on Stephen's romantic self-indulgence. As the young man attempts to "still the riot of his blood," he swoons in languorous ecstasy. He poetically envisions an "opening flower": "Glimmering and trembling, trembling and unfolding, a breaking light, . . . it spread in endless succession to itself, breaking in full crimson and unfolding and fading to palest rose, leaf by leaf and wave of light by wave of light, flooding all the heavens with its soft flushes, every flush deeper than other."

Sublimating the sexual component of his experience, Stephen vividly imagines a metaphorical rose engulfing the heavens. Certainly, to readers familiar with the psychology of Freud and the poetry of D. H. Lawrence, this "language of flowers" suggests an exercise in erotic displacement. The boy's fantasy re-creates a repressed vision of the female genitalia, spreading in luxuriant rose-pink petals before the aroused male consciousness. Stephen's active libido summons images of a woman's body erotically revealing its sexual mysteries and palpitating with the "crimson flush" of physical stimulation. His florid prose imitates the orgasmic rhythms of sexual excitement, as tension mounts until the dream climaxes in a flood of "soft flushes." Stephen may believe that he has purified his sensuous encounter by making it into an object of art. But even his Dantesque vision is founded on sexual passion, thinly disguised by the language of romantic sublimation.

FLIGHT FROM THE MOTHER

The gates of salvation open at the end of chapter 4. In chapter 5, Stephen finds himself exiled from the Garden of Eden. Chewing crusts of fried bread, he remembers the turf-coloured water in the bath at Clongowes—a spectral image that resonates with associations of death, drowning, and claustrophobia.

The young artist escapes from the sordid reality of Dublin by taking shelter in a world of words. His soul is struggling to fly beyond the nets of family, nationality, and religion. As Stephen proclaims his proud *Non Serviam,* however, he continues to rely on his mother for service and for nurturance. Mary Dedalus washes her son's face and ears, enjoins him to receive communion, and packs his second-hand clothes in preparation for his journey. Having magically transmuted the power of the female into a static object of art, Stephen is again accosted by harsh reminders of Mother Church and Mother Ireland. And so he feels compelled to reject all three "mothers"—physical, spiritual, and political. His refusal to take communion at Easter is as much a gesture of liberation from the pleas of Mary Dedalus as it is a rejection of ecclesiastical authority. The image of woman metonymically absorbs all the paralyzing nets that constrain the artist. Hence Stephen's rejection of Cranly's romantic exaltation of "mother love." Unlike his companion, Stephen resolves to detach himself from "the sufferings of women, the weaknesses of their bodies and souls"; he refuses to "shield them with a strong and resolute arm and bow his mind to them." He determines, instead, to "discover the mode of life or of art" that will allow his spirit to "express itself in unfettered freedom." In casting off the yoke of matriarchy, Stephen asserts his manhood in fraternal collusion with Daedalus, his classical mentor.

The male artistic spirit is symbolized by birds that wheel above the sensuous world and become emblems of a disembodied consciousness. Like Swedenborg, Stephen is convinced of "the correspondence of birds to things of the intellect." Swallows careening in the evening air become symbols of the unfettered spirit of the male artist. The female, in contrast, is depicted either as a water bird, immersed in the fluidity of sensuous life, or as a "batlike" creature mired in the dark secrets of a primitive race. The peasant woman who solicits Davin resembles a mysterious sprite out of Celtic folklore, "a batlike soul waking to the consciousness of itself in darkness and secrecy and loneliness and, through the eyes and voice and gesture of a woman without guile, calling the stranger to her bed." Similarly, when Emma shows interest in Father Moran and the Irish Renascence, she becomes a virginal Kathleen ni Houlihan, another "batlike soul . . . tarrying awhile, loveless and sinless."

It is not enough to repudiate the female. The artist must usurp her procreative powers. Stephen seems to consider the aesthetic endeavor a kind of "couvade"—a rite of psychological compensation for the male's inability to give birth. He describes the act of aesthetic "postcreation" in metaphors of parturition, explaining to Lynch: "When we come to the phenomena of artistic conception, artistic gestation, and artistic reproduction I require a new terminology and a new personal experience."

When Stephen awakens to "a tremulous morning knowledge, a morning inspiration," his experience is oddly passive: "A spirit filled him, pure as the purest water, sweet as dew, moving as music. But how faintly it was inbreathed, how passionlessly, as if the seraphim themselves were breathing upon him!" It soon becomes clear that it is not simply the seraphim who are breathing upon the artist, but the Holy Ghost, in an aesthetic drama that reenacts the mystery of Christ's Incarnation. The poet welters in a confused haze of light and beauty, but the "instant of inspiration" is climactic: "O! In the virgin womb of the imagination the word was made flesh. Gabriel the seraph had come to the virgin's chamber."

In a strange instance of mental transsexuality, Stephen identifies with the Blessed Virgin Mary, to whom the angel Gabriel announced the conception of Christ. The virginal imagination becomes hand-maid to the Lord, echoing Mary's words: "Be it done unto me according to thy word." Stephen here suggests a fleshly embodiment of the divine word through an "immaculate conception" in the mind of the poet. He assumes that the artist can engender "life out of life" through an exclusively spiritual process. The imagination is impregnated by the seminal lightning of the Holy Ghost. It then gives birth to the word incarnate in art—or perhaps, as Stephen fails to understand, to a stillbirth untouched by the vitalizing forces of physical reality. So long as the aesthetic consciousness remains virginal, it fails to conceive works of art that reflect the life of the outer world.

Despite the apparent sophistication of Stephen's aesthetic theory in *A Portrait,* the virgin womb of his imagination has yet to be fertilized by external experience. The artist's talents are woefully incommensurate with his idealistic conceptions. Inspired by masturbatory fantasies after a wet dream, Stephen pens the "Villanelle of a Temptress," a mediocre poem that conflates profane and religious imagery in a hymn of praise to the seductive muse. Emma, his model, is once again transmuted by lyrical stasis. Stephen identifies the "rose and ardent light" of inspiration with her strange and "wilfull heart, strange that no man had known or would know, wilful from before the beginning of the world." Emma merges with all the sirens and beautiful women of religious history and myth— with the Virgin Mary, with Dante's Beatrice, and with the "secret rose" of Yeats's early poetry.

Stephen bitterly speculates that Emma has prostituted herself to the Irish Renascence and to a "church which was the scullerymaid of christendom." "Rude brutal anger" fragments her image in a kaleidoscope of sordid memories. Emma, however, is never allowed to defend herself. Stephen sets himself up as all-seeing judge, surmising and speculating about Emma's change of heart, but contemptuous of direct communication with his putative betrayer. He feels angry that she will confess her sins to the vulgar Father Moran, a "priested peasant," rather than to Stephen, "a priest of eternal imagination, transmuting the daily bread of experience into the radiant body of everliving life."

Stephen thinks of Emma with a curious mixture of homage and disdain. He mingles love with lust, religious worship with lascivious desire. In his sexual fantasies, Emma yields her warm, naked body to his amorous embrace. "Conscious of his desire she was waking from odorous sleep, the temptress of his villanelle. . . . Her nakedness yielded to him, radiant, warm, odorous and lavish-limbed, enfolded him like a shining cloud, enfolded him like water with a liquid life." Emma is seductress and muse, Blessed Mother and aesthetic siren, whose "waters circumfluent in space" engender the "liquid letters" of poetic speech, "symbols of the element of mystery." Here female fluidity becomes essential to art, and the eternal temptress baptizes the nascent poet with the gift of lyrical utterance.

Does Emma fade out of the novel as the temptress of Stephen's villanelle? Does she "lure the seraphim" and have her will of man through *"languorous look and lavish limb"*? This is hardly the Emma we recognize from the novel. The formal, highly wrought verses of Stephen's poem reveal his perpetual obsession with the terrifying eroticism of the female. Art enables him temporarily to control the archetypal seductress, whose *"eyes have set man's heart ablaze"* from the beginning of time. Against overwhelming enchantment, Stephen pits the forces of aesthetic transformation. As poet-priest, he transubstantiates the eternal feminine into a static, disembodied muse. Once out of nature, the Circean figure ceases to threaten. Consigned to the realm of Byzantium, she can no longer arouse animal lust or sensuous passion. The seductive female is safely embalmed and held suspended in the "everliving life" of art.

Throughout *A Portrait,* Stephen habitually makes use of poetry to sublimate personal emotions of rage, jealousy, and desire. Suspecting Emma of a liaison with Cranly, he imagines an illicit affair between the two, then calms himself by uttering some misremembered lines from Nash: *"Darkness falls from the air."* Filled with excitement as Emma passes, Stephen cannot decide whether his emotion is erotically or lyrically inspired: "A trembling joy, lambent as a faint light, played like a fairy host around him. But why? Her passage through the darkening air or the verse with its black vowels and its opening sound, rich and lutelike?" After a scatological meditation on life in Stuart England, Stephen responds to Emma's presence like an animal scenting its prey: "Vaguely first and then more sharply he smelt her body. A conscious unrest seethed in his blood. Yes, it was her body he smelt: a wild and languid smell." Aroused and unsatisfied, comforted neither by woman nor by verse, the louse-ridden poet abandons his pursuit: "Well, then, let her go and be damned to her. She could love some clean athlete who washed himself every morning to the waist and had black hair on his chest. Let her." Stephen's rejection of Emma is not without a touch of self-pity. He thinks mournfully: "But him no woman's eyes had wooed."

Even a servant girl singing "Rosie O'Grady" is transmuted in Stephen's mind into an ephemeral image of liturgical incantation: "The figure of woman as she appears in the liturgy of the church passed silently through the darkness: a whiterobed figure, small and slender as a boy and with a falling girdle." The androgynous phantasm, with a voice "frail and high as a boy's," intones a passage out of the Bible. Stephen's mind is immersed in the aesthetic beauty of ecclesiastical rites. He protests that he cannot place his faith in the "real love" associated with "sweet Rosie O'Grady" until he first sees the enigmatic Rosie. True love between man and woman may, indeed, be nothing but a chimera of the romantic imagination.

Toward the end of the novel, Stephen's Platonic musings give way to flippant remarks and lewd jokes. In the company of Lynch, he follows a "sizable hospital nurse" and comments on her cow-like proportions. The young men resemble two "lean hungry greyhounds walking after a heifer." The "wild spring" brings Stephen's roving eye to rest on girls "demure and romping. All fair or auburn:

no dark ones. They blush better." The motif of shame and humili-ation continues to inform his thoughts about women. He feels pity for Emma, "humbled and saddened by the dark shame of woman-hood," and equates menstruation with a fall from innocence. He remarks facetiously that, according to Lynch, statues of women "should always be fully draped, one hand of the woman feeling regretfully her own hinder parts." In Stephen's mind, the female is "shame-wounded" by nature, bovine and buttocks-bound, chafing from the scatological burdens of bodily process.

In his final meeting with Emma, Stephen freezes her image in the guise of an idealized Beatrice by opening the "spiritual-heroic refrigerating apparatus, invented and patented in all countries by Dante Alighieri." He concedes in his diary: "Yes, I liked her today." But the seeds of friendship or affection will not be allowed to ripen. Rejecting the arms of women, Stephen chooses "the white arms of roads, their promise of close embraces and the black arms of tall ships that stand against the moon, their tale of distant nations."

Throughout *A Portrait,* Stephen has manifested a psychological horror of the female as a figure of immanence, a symbol of physical temptation, and a perpetual reminder of mortality. At the end of the novel, he flees from all the women who have served as catalysts in his own growth. His journey into exile will release him from what he perceives as a cloying matriarchal authority. He must blot from his ears "his mother's sobs and reproaches" and strike from his eyes the insistent "image of his mother's face." Alone and proud, isolated and free, Stephen proclaims joyful allegiance to the masculine fraternity of Daedalus, his priest and patron: "Welcome, O life! I go to encounter for the millionth time the reality of experience and to forge in the smithy of my soul the uncreated conscience of my race. . . . Old father, old artificer, stand me now and ever in good stead." The hyperbolic resonance of Stephen's invocation leads us to suspect that his fate will be Icarian rather than Daedalian. Insofar as women are concerned, he goes to encounter the "reality of experi-ence" not for the millionth time, but for the first.

Joyce's protagonist has constantly tried to achieve mastery over the outer world by adopting a male model of aesthetic creation. In the very act of "word-shaping," he can impose his will on a resistant environment and reduce the chaotic fluidity of life to the controlled stasis of art. Much of the irony in *A Portrait,* however, results from Joyce's satire of Stephen's logocentric paradigm. The hero naively gathers phrases for his "word-hoard" without infusing his "capful of light odes" (*Ulysses*) with the spark of human sympathy.

Certainly, the reader may feel baffled or uneasy about the degree of irony implicit in Joyce's portrait of the artist as a young man. To what extent is the author gently mocking his character in a fictional exposure of adolescent narcissism? There is a great deal of evidence in *A Portrait* that Stephen's misogyny is, in fact, still another example of his youthful priggishness. The pervasive irony that tinges the hero's scrupulous devotions and gives his aesthetic theory that "true scholastic stink" surely informs his relations with women—from his mother and Dante Riordan to Emma and the unnamed bird-girl he idealizes on the beach. Joyce makes clear to his audience that Stephen's fear of woman and contempt for sensuous life are among the many inhibitions that stifle his creativity. Before he can become a priest of the eternal imagination, Stephen must first divest himself of the "spiritual-heroic refrigerating apparatus" that characterizes the egocentric aesthete. Misogyny is one of the adolescent traits he has to outgrow on the path to artistic maturity. Not until *Ulysses* will a new model begin to emerge—one that recognizes the need for the intellectual artist to "make his peace" with woman and to incorporate into his work the vital, semiotic flow of female life.

The Beauty of Mortal Conditions: Joyce's *A Portrait of the Artist*

Martin Price

"Sceptically, cynically, mystically, he had sought for an absolute satisfaction and now little by little he began to be conscious of the beauty of mortal conditions."

The sentence is from the sketch which was Joyce's earliest version of his portrait of the artist. It reveals some of the difficulty of that process by which the work of art emerges from the conditions of its creation and the artist from the natural man. Artistic creation may be one of the ways of most fully realizing the self, but it is achieved only as the artist is freed of impediments within the self and of exigencies outside. And yet the problem of liberation is a subtle one; for the artist may too easily be delivered of much that makes him human and gives his experience depth.

Joyce provides us with an amusing illustration of that danger. Stephen Dedalus, having attained a state of spiritual exaltation, finds in himself a serene transcendence:

The world for all its solid substance and complexity no longer existed for his soul save as a theorem of divine power and love and universality. So entire and unquestionable was this sense of the divine meaning in all nature granted to his soul that he could scarcely understand why it was in any way necessary that he should continue to live.

From *Forms of Life*. © 1983 by Yale University. Yale University Press, 1983.

This pitch of spirituality cannot be sustained very long. It is an episode in the longer process that Joyce traces from the earliest sensory and associative images to the full powers of mind as they are shown in the creation of a poem and the enunciation of an aesthetic. Even those achievements are stages in the process that culminates (to use Richard Ellmann's phrase) in "the gestation of a soul," in the emergence of the artist from—or better, in—the young man. This final state is achieved by a fuller consciousness; and by its very nature it is joined to the world.

It is with that process that I shall be concerned in this chapter. It is a process in which form emerges from the conditions which have given rise to it, that is, either created the form or called it forth. The form cannot free itself too completely from those conditions lest it lose the very point of its existence. One of the appeals of literary realism, in which it shows a resemblance to history, is its recognition of a stubborn and resistant world of fact, from which events or patterns cannot be easily exacted. For this resistance must be more than dialectical; it cannot be dissolved by an act of the mind. After we have come to recognize the categories which our thought must impose and the work of interpretation that is implicit in our experience (as opposed to innocent eyes and brute facts) there is still an unaccommodating otherness with which the artist must negotiate or struggle if his art is to be brought to power. The work of art embodies some memory of or allusion to the conditions that attend on and perhaps all but prevent its existence.

These conditions, once they have ceased to be a threat to the pure idea and have been assumed into the work of art, may yield up their beauty in unforeseen ways. We have seen something of this occur in many of the novelists I have discussed. I should like to cite one more analogy from painting. It is drawn from a discussion of Cézanne's landscapes by Meyer Schapiro. Instead of imposing an "ideal schema," Cézanne achieves a "more complex relationship emerging slowly in the course of the work. The form is in constant making and contributes an aspect of the encountered and random to the full appearance of the scene, inviting us to endless exploration." The "encountered and random," or as Schapiro puts it a page or two earlier, "the aspect of chance in the appearance of directly encountered things," suggests the unassimilable world of fact, with all its contingency and indifference to idea. It is a theme of Iris Murdoch's writing, too: "The great artists reveal the detail of the world." We can almost say that the value of form is less the order it creates than the way it heightens those details which resist it. "The pointlessness of art is not the pointlessness of a game; it is the pointlessness of human life itself, and form in art is properly the simulation of the self-contained aimlessness of the universe." What this emphasis brings to our awareness is the peculiar intensity that the novel can lend a detail, a gesture, an event—not by loading it with symbolic import but by giving us the sense of what it is to see such detail when it is rich with the possibility of meanings, no one of which has yet been precipitated or asserted.

The first chapter of the *Portrait* concludes with Stephen's first act of self-assertion. It is an act of heroism if not defiance, a firm insistence upon justice against the Jesuit headmaster's casual dismissal of Father Dolan's cruelty. And while Stephen is later to learn of the "hearty laugh" his elders had over his protest, at the moment he can feel only triumph in his return down the lonely corridor to be chaired by his fellow students. But if a self has begun to be defined, it is still to be tested in Stephen's battle "against the squalor of his life and spirit" and "the riot of his mind." The instability of Dedalus family life, the "changes in what he had deemed unchangeable," deflect Stephen from the world about him to one of daydream, of an imagined meeting with "the unsubstantial image . . . his soul so constantly beheld." The meeting is to be release and transfiguration: "Weakness and timidity and inexperience would fall from him in that magic moment." But, in fact, the passivity of expectation afflicts him with a kind of paralysis.

At school, Stephen shows a mixture of defiant assertion and humiliating compliance, of heretical beliefs and "habits of quiet obedience." (The deadlock creates a riot of brutal passion in his imagination, consequent guilt and horror with himself, and withdrawal from others.) "By his monstrous way of life he seemed to have put himself beyond the limits of reality. Nothing moved him or spoke to him from the real world unless he heard in it an echo of the infuriated cries within him."

Joyce treats Stephen with little irony during this season of torment. The release is not yet transfiguration. There is no holy encounter with a romantic heroine, but instead the surrender to a prostitute whose tongue he feels upon his own as "an unknown and timid pressure, darker than the swoon of sin, softer than sound or odour." Self-destruction seems inextricably tied to necessary self-assertion: "It was his own soul going forth to experience, unfolding itself sin by sin, spreading abroad the balefire of its burning stars and folding back upon itself, fading slowly, quenching its own lights and fires."

Throughout the second and third chapters Joyce creates an undertone of comic disproportion between Stephen's view of his sins and the appearance they present to us. There are wonderfully subtle doubts Stephen can propound through curious and ingenious questions. There are fantasies in which he has submitted Emma to "his brutelike lust . . . and trampled upon her innocence." There are indecent pictures he has drawn and obscene letters he has inscribed and scattered to be found by passersby. The intensity of self-excoriation these actions induce finds its relief in a sentimental fantasy of forgiveness and reward. He dares not approach God or even Mary directly, but he draws Emma beside him (involving her in more complicity than is in fact her due) in a "wide land under a tender lucid evening sky." Mary becomes the all-forgiving mother of "children that had erred" and confers Emma's heart upon him in the process: "Take hands, Stephen and Emma. It is a beautiful evening now in heaven. You have erred but you are always my children. It is one heart that loves another heart. Take hands together, my dear children, and you will be happy together and your hearts will love each other."

If the sentimental forgiveness is one extreme, the Bosch-like fantasies of fiends mocking with terrifying gibberish or of goatish monsters encircling him in a filthy field are the other. The disproportion between fantasy and actuality creates an ironic space around Stephen's anguish. When at last he makes confession in a strange church, the priest's formulaic questions are too general and inclusive for the uniquely terrible sin that Stephen feels he has committed:

> —I . . . committed sins of impurity, father.
> The priest did not turn his head.
> —With yourself, my child?
> —And . . . with others.
> —With women, my child?
> —Yes, father.
> —Were they married women, my child?
> He did not know. His sins trickled from his lips, one by

one, trickled in shameful drops from his soul festering and oozing like a sore, a squalid stream of vice.

Again, after his purgation, Stephen's religious devotion becomes brilliantly callow, and he anticipates Samuel Beckett's heroes in a number of ways.

> By means of ejaculations and prayers he stored up ungrudgingly for souls in purgatory centuries of days and quarantines and years; yet the spiritual triumph which he felt in achieving with ease so many fabulous ages of canonical penances did not wholly reward his goal of prayer since he could never learn how much temporal punishment he had remitted by way of suffrage for the agonising souls.

That note of arithmetical literalness is splendidly deflating, as is the embarrassment of flesh that cannot easily be mortified: "To mortify his smell was more difficult as he found in himself no instinctive repugnance to bad odours, whether they were the odours of the outdoor world such as those of dung and tar or the odours of his own person among which he had made many curious comparisons and experiments." But, of course, protracted selflessness somehow gives rise to irritability and anger; the new assurance of grace begets the anxiety that he may have "really fallen unawares."

The irony that surrounds Stephen's religious dedication prepares for the scene in which he rejects a priestly vocation. The inauthenticity and suppressions that have marked his own devotions reappear for him in the imagined Jesuit's face, "shot with pink tinges of suffocated anger." The scene turns on a resurgence of self. Stephen accepts his "destiny to be elusive of social or religious orders," to "learn his own wisdom apart from others." The fall he dreaded earlier now seems inevitable; and he commits himself to the natural world, "the misrule and confusion of his father's house and the stagnation of vegetable life." At home he hears a sad choir of family voices, singing as they await still another move for a cheaper rent. Stephen listens "to the overtone of weariness behind their frail fresh innocent voices," and the voices open into "an endless reverberation of the choirs of endless generations of children," giving utterance (in Newman's words) to "pain and weariness yet hope for better things."

It is on the shore that Stephen's vocation is made clear: "The artist forging out of the sluggish matter of the earth a new soaring impalpable imperishable being." He imagines himself soaring upward, "delivered of incertitude and made radiant and commingled with the element of the spirit." As he walks alone on the shore, he has overcome passivity and emerged from the "house of squalor and subterfuge." It is then that he sees the girl who carries in her form all the suggestion of romantic heroines, of Emma, of the Virgin, and, most of all, of "the beauty of mortal conditions."

In the final chapter of the novel, Joyce sets forth the claims upon Stephen of both church and nation and meets them with the vocation of the artist. Ireland has become a constellation of demands and affronts, and Stephen sees its debasement in the statute of Tom Moore, the "national poet": "He looked at it without anger: for, though sloth of the body and of the soul crept over it like unseen vermin, over the shuffling feet and up the folds of the cloak and around the servile head, it seemed humbly unconscious of its indignity." Stephen is reminded of Davin, "the peasant student," "one of the tame geese," regarding Ireland with the same uncritical acceptance he shows for the Roman Catholic religion, "the attitude of a dullwitted loyal serf." Davin in turn evokes the Irish peasant woman who invited him to her bed, a "type of her race and his own, a bat-like soul waking to the consciousness of itself in darkness and secrecy and loneliness." At every point Stephen opposes the Irish scene with associations that come from elsewhere—Newman, Cavalcanti, Ibsen, Jonson. "Try to be one of us," Davin asks. "In your heart you are an Irishman but your pride is too powerful." But Stephen must see Ireland's claims as captivity: "When the soul of a man is born in this country there are nets flung at it to hold it back from flight. You talk to me of nationality, language, religion. I shall try to fly by those nets." He parries the claims that his friend Cranly advances in Ireland's behalf, the most compelling of them Stephen's mother's wish that he remain in the faith. "Whatever she feels, it, at least, must be real," Cranly insists. "It must be. What are our ideas or ambitions? Play. Ideas!" Cranly asserts that Stephen has more religious faith than he knows, that his doubts are only an expression of that faith. And it is through his replies to Cranly that Stephen extricates himself from all the claims made upon him: "I will not serve that in which I no longer believe whether it call itself my home, my fatherland or my church: and I will try to express myself in some mode of life or art as freely as I can and as wholly as I can, using for my defence the only arms I allow myself to use—silence, exile, and cunning."

The aesthetic Stephen formulates is a culmination of this movement toward freedom. It is not an assertion of the purity of art but of its autonomy. Out of the natural feelings there emerges a peculiar "aesthetic emotion," not so much a distinct kind as a distinct form of emotion. The feelings of practical life—kinetic, concerned with possession or avoidance but in either case with motion—undergo an "arrest."

It is in such moments of arrest that we enter a "mental world." We are beyond the "purely reflex action of the nervous system" and reach a realm of free contemplation, an "esthetic stasis" in which we feel no excitation to action, but rather "an ideal pity or an ideal terror." This stasis is experience framed, discontinuous with the stream of ordinary feelings; the framing is achieved by aesthetic form—"the rhythm of beauty." Stephen states the freedom of the aesthetic response with mock-solemnity: we "try slowly and humbly and constantly to express, to press out again, from the gross earth or what it brings forth [Lynch has amiably protested, "please remember, though I did eat a cake of cowdung once, that I admire only beauty"], from sound and shape and colour which are the prison gates of our soul, an image of the beauty we have come to understand—that is art." Stephen (and certainly Joyce) is too much the Aristotelian to speak of the objects of the senses as the "prison gates of our soul" except with a certain ironic exaggeration. He is perhaps stirred by Lynch's grossness to insist upon the cognitive, upon an intellectual beauty that contrasts with sensory impressions. But as he speaks, the novelist insists in turn upon the concreteness of the physical world: "They had reached the canal bridge and, turning from their course, went on by the trees. A crude grey light, mirrored in the sluggish water, and a smell of wet branches over their heads seemed to war against the course of Stephen's thought."

Stephen's definition of art includes the senses as much as the intellect: it is "the human disposition of sensible or intelligible matter for an esthetic end." What matters is that both are liberated from the practical, the moral, the kinetic; if the immediate object of beauty is pleasure, it remains indifferent to judgments of good and evil. Stephen is freeing the work of art as he is freeing himself from the claims that are being pressed upon both—duty to church and to country. The aesthetic becomes a privileged experience: it has autonomy within its own province, and it has the duty to itself, as it were, of becoming a work of art, just as Stephen owes himself the initial duty of becoming an artist.

While Stephen adamantly asserts the autonomy of art and the transfiguration of natural experience into the work of imagination ("Life purified in and reprojected from the human imagination"), he does not expound a doctrine of Art for Art's Sake. He is dedicated to freeing art of its captivity by typical "natural pieties—social limitations, inherited apathy of race, an adoring mother, the Christian fable." Joyce himself had no esteem for the Celtic revival, for hermeticism and magic, for "the union of faith and fatherland." As he wrote in "Drama and Life," the first paper he read aloud at a college society, "Art is marred by . . . mistaken insistence on its religious, its moral, its beautiful, its idealizing tendencies. A single Rembrandt is worth a gallery full of Van Dycks." Idealism and romance are to be avoided. "Life we must accept as we see it before our eyes, men and women as we meet them in the real world, not as we apprehend them in the world of faery."

One finds in the young Joyce as in Stephen the wish to use art as a means of restoring nobility to Ireland. "I am an enemy of the ignobleness and slavishness of people but not of you," Joyce wrote to Nora (August 29, 1904). At about the same time in his earliest version of the *Portrait,* Joyce described his character (or himself) as "at the difficult age, dispossessed and necessitous, sensible of all that was ignoble in such manners [of his contemporaries] who, in revery at least, had been acquainted with nobility." So Ireland's one belief is "in the incurable ignobility of the forces that have overcome her." One thinks of the "breakwater of order and elegance" the young Stephen tries to build, the "squalor and subterfuge" he wants to put behind him. By the end of the novel, he has come to a vision of what his art may achieve. This emerges from the bitterness with which he regards the "sleek lives of the patricians of Ireland," squandering their authority in acquisitiveness and triviality:

> How could he hit their conscience or how cast his shadow
> over the imaginations of their daughters, before their
> squires begat upon them, that they might breed a race less
> ignoble than their own? And under the deepened dusk he
> felt the thoughts and desires of the race to which he

belonged flitting like bats, across the dark country lanes, under trees by the edges of streams and near the pool-mottled bogs.

But to achieve such a purpose, he must first of all become an artist.

The composition of a poem turns this process so theoretically expounded into fallible actuality. The villanelle emerges from inchoate feeling. The "morning knowledge" to which Stephen awakens is a state of purity; and only gradually, under the stress of recall, Stephen moves from seraphic ecstasy to erotic fantasy, from the sense of himself as passionless spirit to the role of Gabriel as the seraph of annunciation, from white flame to rose and ardent light, from the seraphim breathing upon him to the choirs of the seraphim falling from heaven, he among them. The willful heart of the actual virgin—Emma Clery—becomes the lure of a temptress worshipped as the Virgin might be, smoke of praise like "incense ascending from the altar of the world." The feelings have so far moved through a stream of associations, and now they are suddenly blocked: "Smoke went up from the whole earth, from the vapoury oceans, smoke of her praise. The earth was like a swinging swaying censer, a ball of incense, an ellipsoidal ball. The rhythm died out at once; the cry of his heart was broken." Broken by the full recollection of the whinnying, centaurlike laughter of Moynihan in the lecture room: "What price ellipsoidal balls! chase me, ladies, I'm in the cavalry." We may recall with pleasure the "sabbath of misrule" of Moynihan's "rude humour"; but Stephen is incapable of absorbing so affronting an aspect of reality. He must free himself of the threat of incongruity; if, as Walter Shandy remarked, "there is no passion so serious as lust," there is no poetry so solemn as its sublimation.

As he writes out the stanzas of the villanelle, Stephen summons up more and more concretely the image of Emma. The "lumps of knotted flesh" in his "lumpy pillow" recall the "lumps of knotted horsehair in the sofa of her parlour on which he used to sit." All his distrust of her is reawakened with her attraction. She is timid, orthodox, given to flirting with the priests, who make her feel safe. Moved to anger by his memories, Stephen summons up girls he has casually encountered, girls whom he has glanced at. Emma becomes, in the process, representative, an embodiment of the secret of her race (like the peasant woman Davin encountered). And, as she is magnified and made more innocently devious, Stephen's competitive sense awakens him to self-assertion against the "priested peasant" she favors. "To him she would unveil her soul's shy nakedness, to one who was but schooled in the discharging of a formal rite rather than to him, a priest of eternal imagination, transmitting the daily bread of experience into the radiant body of everlasting life." The triumphant vision of himself as priest of imagination makes his poem a "eucharistic hymn," and the transubstantiation of feeling into art has been accomplished. Almost. For, moved by the renewal of his poetry, of his capacity to honor her in verses again, he comes to a more generous vision of her innocence, to a more hopeful dream of her responsiveness. And finally the associations move to their inevitable culmination: a fantasy of erotic fulfillment. "Her naked-ness yielded to him, radiant, warm, odorous, and lavishlimbed," and the poem comes to its completion: "like a cloud of vapour or like waters circumfluent in space the liquid letters of speech, symbols of the element of mystery, flowed forth over his brain."

The villanelle is of less interest than the process of composition itself. That a poem emerges we are sufficiently persuaded; and the form of the villanelle insists upon its artfulness. That the poem is in large measure traceable to erotic fantasy and yet freed of Stephen's experience as it stands on the page is the point of the process. A finer poem might leave the associations of feeling further behind, espe-cially if it were achieved by subtler and tighter thought than this poem has demanded. This transfiguration is, in short, not so complete as to transcend its sources; it can be seen in process and recapitulates the aesthetic argument that has preceded it. But that is Joyce's purpose, which a better poem might not serve so well.

The book ends with Stephen freed—not without doubts, second thoughts, regrets—to leave Ireland and to embrace "the loveliness which has not yet come into the world." He turns away from what might seem aestheticism, for his conception of art is more strenuous and severe. "I go to encounter for the millionth time and to forge in the smithy of my soul the uncreated conscience of my race." As the artist has emerged from the young man, so the conscience of Ireland may emerge from the artist. It is a high calling, no mean or middle flight.

The Preposterous Shape of Portraiture: *A Portrait of the Artist as a Young Man*

John Paul Riquelme

> *Formally the novel is close to the dream; both can be defined by consideration of this curious property: all their deviations form part of them.*
> PAUL VALÉRY

> *The genius in the act of creation . . . resembles the uncanny fairy tale image which is able to see itself by turning its eyes. He is at once subject and object, poet, actor, and audience.*
> NIETZSCHE, *The Birth of Tragedy*

OSCILLATING PERSPECTIVE

In my commentary on *Finnegans Wake,* I explain how Joyce provides the reader in various ways with the means for achieving an oscillating perspective. That perspective is a viewpoint for reading that vacillates between mutually defining poles, just as our perception of the relation between figure and ground in some optical illusions may shift. The vacillating viewpoint is available in Joyce's writing much earlier than the *Wake,* as early, in fact, as *A Portrait of the Artist as a Young Man.* Joyce creates it through style in the continuing refinement of his techniques for rendering consciousness that he develops during the writing of *Dubliners* and *Stephen Hero.* The subtle intermingling of third- and first-person perspectives that Joyce effects in

From *Teller and Tale in Joyce's Fiction: Oscillating Perspectives.* © 1983 by the Johns Hopkins University Press, Baltimore/London.

A Portrait is the most significant change in the style of his autobiographical work, one that differentiates it clearly from *Stephen Hero.*
The mixing of narrator's and character's views and voices in *A
Portrait,* which is prepared for by aspects of *Dubliners,* will become
the donnée of *Ulysses,* the stylistic element the later work starts with,
deviates from, then returns to in "Penelope." It is also an early step
toward the radical superimposing of voices in *Finnegans Wake.*

In addition, Joyce encourages the oscillating perspective in *A
Portrait* by constructing his narrative to avoid the pretense that his
narration is a transparent vehicle for plot. He eschews that pretense
through subverting the conventions of realism. Generally speaking,
in fiction those conventions, including a single telling voice or style
and a coherent chronological presentation, are undercut when the
narration includes apparently heterogeneous material: diagrams,
documents, or stories-within-the-text. Joyce achieves some of his
most arresting and puzzling effects in *A Portrait* by injecting heterogeneous elements into the narrative. By disrupting the semblance of
a continuous flow of narrative, these elements draw attention to the
book's artifice, to its status as art, and to themselves as relatively
independent of the text containing them. These aspects of narrative
can function similarly to the epic similes in *Paradise Lost* as Geoffrey
Hartman has described them ("Milton's Counterplot," in *Milton: A
Collection of Critical Essays,* ed. Louis L. Martz). They set up
countermovements in the reading process that may engender an
oscillating perspective on the totality of the work's details.

In this regard, Joyce's autobiographical fiction resembles another
eccentric work, a fictional autobiography, Laurence Sterne's *Tristram
Shandy.* Sterne's book is one of the most famous heterogeneous
instances in the history of fiction, in part because the narrator's
divagations distract the reader repeatedly from any passive response
to the text based on unquestioned assumptions about what a novel
should be and what its implications may legitimately include.
Sterne's book contains blank, black, and marbled pages, as well as
ellipses, diagrams, and a musical score. The narrator quotes at length
from documents such as his parents' marriage contract. He prints *en
face* an English translation of a story written in Latin by Hafen
Slawkenbergius, a fictitious author. Because of their styles and
structures these divergences from what Tristram calls the straight
line of the narrative encourage the reader to reflect on the various
styles and structures of the larger work providing their context. Text

as whole and internal segment as part become mutually defining. The part differs radically from its context, but both part and context contribute to the whole that is the narrative.

Such elements as the title and the epigraphs in *Tristram Shandy* tend to create perspectives for the reader that raise problems about how to understand the novel in its parts and in its totality. The full title, *The Life and Opinions of Tristram Shandy, Gentleman,* indicates that within the covers of the book can be found the central character's life and opinions. But the title is at odds with the narrative, for much of the novel presents material from before the time Tristram and his opinions supposedly come into existence. By trying to fill in background and past history, Tristram as narrator is hardly ever able to present himself as character, is almost never able to write about the present or the recent past relative to the time of his act of writing. That act of writing itself, as well as the subjects being written about, becomes an important focus of the reader's attention and of Tristram's. Of the various epigraphs affixed to the volumes of *Tristram Shandy,* the one ascribed to Pliny the Younger at the head of volume seven suggests most clearly a possible interpretation for the form of the narration with its numerous digressions and embellishments. Even though volume seven swerves from the narrative immediately preceding it by presenting unexpected subject matter, the epigraph states in Latin that "this is not an excursion from it, but is the work itself." The oddities of the narration can create an essential frame of reference for interpreting the text containing them.

Although Joyce's *A Portrait of the Artist as a Young Man* is neither as obviously idiosyncratic as *Tristram Shandy* nor as unusual as Joyce's later fictions, like them, it is only marginally a *novel,* if by that term we mean a prose narration that abides by the canons of realism. These works include elements of form revealing disequilibria in the conventions of the telling that are startling and, at times, disquieting. In *A Portrait* the disturbing elements that raise the question of the book's marginal status are most prominent at the beginning and the ending. These are the locations of the text's margins, its borders with a world not delimited by the language of the story. Title, epigraph, and journal are the gates into and out of Joyce's work. They provide for the reader portals of discovery, margins to be negotiated and filled during the reading process.

These parts of *A Portrait* and many of the anomalies that characterize similar texts are analogous to an element Freud claims is present in every dream. In what must be the most unusual footnote in *The Interpretation of Dreams,* a book full of curiosities, Freud asserts that "there is at least one spot in every dream at which it is unplumbable—a navel, as it were, that is its point of contact with the unknown." The navel is the point at which the umbilical cord has been cut. It suggests simultaneously the connection and the severing of the connection between parent and child, or, in aesthetic terms, between creator and artifact. It is both the mark or signature of the creator's activity and the sign of the creation's autonomy. As point of contact with the unknown, the navel of the dream cannot be completely apprehended through the logic of propositions either because evidence is insufficient for a determinate conclusion or because some paradox preempts the efficacy of conventional logic. The navel is the mark of the conundrum, of what can be known only marginally, not fully or directly. Both Freud's essay and Joyce's book depend on pretexts—on ruses and on previously existing works. Through its form, each announces itself to be a revision of prior texts, particularly ones by the writer, which are either displaced or included within the text we read. In Freud's essay the process of revision is indicated by multiple references to previous editions, parts of which have been reprinted, others deleted, still others recast in the production of subsequent versions. Freud's pretext for writing his volume, to illuminate the nature of dreams and dreaming, disguises a book that is not primarily about the originating process of dreaming but instead focuses on the belated process of interpretation.

A Portrait also contains numerous references to other texts, including poems, stories, novels, and diaries, that exist earlier than itself either in actuality or in the fiction of the narrative's chronology. The book is the revision of these previous texts contained either wholly or partially within it. Here Joyce anticipates the procedure of his later works. As in [*Finnegans*] *Wake,* in *A Portrait,* the artist's activity is essentially rewriting. Joyce indicates within the text the task performed by every serious writer: the act of revision that is at once the author's writing and reading (as interpretation) of his self-made image in language. Like the narrator of Proust's *Remembrance of Things Past,* who touches up his earlier work before including it in the novel, Joyce as teller engages in the continuing work of revising the book of himself. Both Proust and Joyce include in their narrations infinitely regressive paradoxes about the relations of life and art. With regard to *A Portrait,* the act of revision, for which the book is evidence, is a crucial but unstated implication of the story's form.

Joyce responds to texts that already exist by rewriting his own earlier work, whether or not published, the work of his predecessors, and occasionally the work of his contemporaries. In the *Wake,* Joyce alludes to and transforms numerous texts by other writers of his period. These include, most prominently, Wyndham Lewis and T. S. Eliot, both of whom had responded in print to *Ulysses.* Lewis's negative comments are well known. Eliot reacted to *Ulysses* by writing his famous review "*Ulysses,* Order, and Myth" and (in Joyce's opinion) *The Waste Land.* Although Joyce's allusions of this kind are, in one sense, autobiographical, their peculiar literary nature makes them something other than simple contributions to our vision of the author's life. Instead, they give us aspects of a general image of both the artist and the creative process, a process that includes within its products responses to its own earlier incarnations.

Many critics who have written on *A Portrait* interpret that work autobiographically, claiming that it is based on details of Joyce's youth. Generally, they adduce the title as evidence for the link between the life and the work of art: the portrait is of the artist who writes the book. Unquestionably, strong evidence supports this kind of autobiographical reading. But an autobiographical interpretation of a different sort is also possible, one that sees Stephen Dedalus as the teller of his own story. When we read Freud on dreams, we learn that the fulfillment of the process of dreaming, another kind of retelling of stories, occurs in the interpretation of dreams, a belated activity in which the dreamer and the analyst may be one. In *A Portrait,* we discover that the fulfillment of the process of becoming an author occurs in the act of writing, a belated activity in which character and narrator may be one. Implicit in the story of Stephen Dedalus's growth to maturity is the process by which his book emerges from previously existing texts that Stephen knows, some of which he has written himself. *A Portrait* is both the author's autobiographical fiction and the autobiography of the fictional character. It provides the portrait of both artists.

Any interpretation that suggests Stephen may be the narrator will take exception to most readings that dwell on the problem of irony, or aesthetic distance, and on the impersonality of the narration. By emphasizing the narrator's invisibility and the would-be dramatic or objective presentation of Stephen, those readings generally fail to account adequately for at least two crucial aspects of *A Portrait:* the narrator's recurring presentation of Stephen's consciousness and the various paradoxes of the narration that make describing the details of the story and its form so difficult. Although there can still be disagreements concerning the precise mix of the narrator's attitudes toward the central character at any given moment in the story, if Stephen narrates, the large problem of his future as an artist can no longer be at issue. If he writes his own tale, the story itself as text provides the strongest possible indication that his choice of vocation will yield more valuable work than the writing he produces within the narrative. And the narration indicates exactly what kind of artist Stephen has become. The teller in *A Portrait,* like the purloined letter of Poe's story, is well hidden out in the open, where anyone who cares to look can find him.

Dislocations in Style and Story

A Portrait of the Artist contains displacements in both narrative and narration, story and telling. The literal displacements include the moves of the Dedalus family from one residence to the next always less attractive abode, compounded with Stephen's displacements from school to school, from Clongowes to Belvedere to University College. "Still another removal," Stephen exclaims to himself during the scene in the kitchen with his siblings at the end of part 4, section 2. In Stephen's boyhood and adolescence, sex and religion replace one another in mutually modifying and mutually defining alternation, until their ultimate displacement through coalescence in Stephen's choice of art as vocation. In the future projected by the book's ending, this last development will be last in the sense of previous. That future may bring a series of further developments, each transforming the last from final to merely previous. Stephen's choice of vocation is accompanied by suggestions of the next physical displacement, his planned departure from Ireland, which will take him eventually not just to Paris, but to Trieste.

Displacements in *A Portrait* are temporal as well as spatial and stylistic as well as literal. The ending indicates that Stephen may be entering a period of more mature adulthood, which will replace his young adulthood, the most recent in a series of states stretching back through adolescence to childhood and infancy. The displacements of style are both those of Stephen as developing artist and of the narrator as mature artist. As William M. Schutte has pointed out, "*Portrait,* like *Ulysses* and *Finnegans Wake,* has no one style." By entwining strands of language into a narrative, the teller of the story reaches back through the past to the origins of Stephen's development as an artist. The reaching back by weaving a thread of narrative is like the process of gazing "in your omphalos" practiced by "mystic monks" (*Ulysses*) on which Stephen muses jokingly in "Proteus." There he imagines placing a phone call to "Edenville," his place of origin, along the "strandentwining cable of all flesh," the navel cord that links us all to the past. By transforming the relatively homogeneous style of *Stephen Hero* into the varying, fluctuating styles of *A Portrait,* Joyce manages to produce a "strandentwining cable" of words linking both writer and character to a literary past as origin.

Although they are less emphatically stressed in Joyce's text, the juxtaposed styles in *A Portrait* function essentially as do the shifting voices of Eliot's *The Waste Land.* They exhibit the individual talent of author and character encountering, fracturing, and reusing the resources of the tradition, simultaneously creating a new voice and revivifying the voices of dead authors. In this way the book anticipates the more flamboyant multiplication of styles in *Ulysses,* especially the chronological replication of styles contained in "Oxen of the Sun." In *A Portrait,* by shifting styles Joyce meets a special challenge: to present a wide variety of stylistic exercises that would simultaneously mark the development of a young character's aesthetic sensibilities and form the basis for the writer's exhibition of his own technical mastery. In the various styles of portraiture we have proof of both the character's aesthetic sensitivity and the narrator's virtuosity. The same language serves two purposes. From time to time Joyce directs his adventure in styles toward culminating passages of discovery and self-revelation in which the heightened language vividly calls attention to the relationship of narrator's skill to character's state of mind. The writing of the villanelle in part 5 will be especially important in this regard for our consideration [elsewhere] of the teller's merging with character in *A Portrait.*

During the displacing of earlier parts of the narrative by later parts, the teller modulates among his different styles of narration, including a "vague, nineteenth-century romanticism," "exalted, almost hysterical lyricism," "workaday prose," and the language of Pater and the decadents. In general, the narration consists of anonymous representations of scene, action, and dialogue in the third person together with the report of Stephen's thoughts, also in the third person. The thoughts of other characters are not reported. This sort of presentation allows Joyce a great deal of flexibility. Modulation from one style to another can be smoothly executed as a shift in the character's thinking within the often relatively unobtrusive framework of third-person narration. Some of the more violent, jarring shifts of style occur at the breaks between typographically demarcated segments of the narrative, between the five parts, and between the nineteen smaller sections making up those parts.

There are so many modulations of style in *A Portrait* that any endeavor to characterize generally the details of narration will prove inadequate in some respects. Part of the work's richness and appeal is a verbal texture so variable that it defeats all attempts at reduction to a simple pattern. But the fluctuations do develop in a general direction as the narrative proceeds. In broad terms, the style shifts from psycho-narration narrowly conceived toward narrated monologue; that is, it moves from the narrator's discourse concerning the character's mind to a presentation that also includes the character's mental discourse rendered as the narrator's language. Occasionally, the narrator employs the technique of quoted monologue, language that we understand as the character's supposedly unmediated mental discourse because it employs first person and present tense. The general distinctions between psycho-narration, quoted monologue, and narrated monologue will emerge as we examine specific passages in *A Portrait*. Each technique affects our stance toward character and teller and our sense of the teller's relationship to the tale. All three occur in the context of third-person narration. While we may want to distinguish between them for the purpose of analysis, they hardly ever occur in complete isolation from one another.

Of the three, the most problematic is the narrated monologue, also known as *erlebte Rede* and as *le style indirect libre,* a technique Joyce would have found in Flaubert. This device involves the rendering of the character's consciousness in the third person and the past tense. Although there may be no explicit announcement of mental process in the narrator's language, we understand the passages as thoughts occurring to the character in the first person and in the present tense. The present time of the action, as opposed to the past time indicated by the narration, is often emphasized by deictic adjectives and adverbs and by demonstrative pronouns, which create a sense of immediacy. Here arises the crucial complication that Joyce develops with such subtlety in both *A Portrait* and *Ulysses*. The reader translates the third person into "I" during the reading process. We speak the character's subjectivity, as do narrator and character in their different ways. The use of third person and past tense indicates a tendency toward a fusion of character's voice with teller's voice. The ambiguous merger of voices makes it difficult, even impossible, for the reader to distinguish between the cunningly combined voices of character and narrator. Because the technique requires the reader to translate third person into first and to attempt discriminations, however difficult, between the merged voices, it necessitates the reader's active recreative rendering of the narration. The reader *performs* the text of narrated monologue with a special kind of involvement because of the device's unusual nature.

Quite frequently, the narrator in *A Portrait* summarizes Stephen's thoughts as psycho-narration employing verbs of consciousness prominently either in the past tense or as infinitives. There are numerous examples from the book's early pages: "felt," "wondered," "to remember," "knew." Occasionally several verbs indicating thought are clustered together. In one paragraph early in part 1 there are six instances of such verbs. In general, in this portion of the narrative, there is little emphasis on the complex combination of voices that appears later. (Some exceptions to this general description are 1.1 and such passages as the paragraph in 1.3 beginning "Why did Mr. Barrett. . . .") The reader can easily distinguish the narrator's discourse about Stephen's thoughts from the presentation of scene and dialogue; for instance, in the alternation between these two complementary aspects of the narration in part 1, section 3, the Christmas dinner. As Stephen grows older, the narrator's techniques for presenting his thoughts change. Verbs denoting mental process still occur but less frequently, and other words connoting thought supplement them. Predicates less directly evocative of consciousness, often together with a prepositional phrase, become the reminders that we have access to Stephen's mind.

In part 2, section 2, when Stephen begins wandering the streets of Dublin alone, the passages describing his adventures contain just as many indicators of thought as do some earlier passages, but the indications are of a different order. Stephen makes a map of the city "in his mind." As he follows physically the routes of this internal map, the verb "to wonder," used before in the past tense, now occurs as a present participle, "wondering." While an explicit reference to mental process is still provided, the transformation of the verb denoting thought from a predicate to a modifier makes the reference less obtrusive. Instead of telling us that Stephen thought, felt, or remembered, the narrator presents Stephen's impressions as they "suggested to him," "wakened again in him," or "grew up within him." As before, the references to thought are clustered together, though they are more muted now. These last three predicates and the two preceding quotations are all from a single paragraph. And the predications of thought, even these muted ones, begin to be supplemented or replaced by a new affective vocabulary presenting mood, as in the phrases "mood of embittered silence" and "angry with himself." Or nouns and verbs not necessarily denoting mental activity, such as "vision" and "chronicled," take on connotations that suggest consciousness because of their use in context.

There are two distinctions implicit in the alternation between scene and psyche that occurs in the work's first sections: the distinction between an external world and the character's mind and between narrator and character. Starting in part 2 both begin to be blurred in various ways. The alternation becomes overlap when the narrator quotes Stephen's thoughts in part 2, section 2, using the same typographical indicator, the dash, that previously identified only direct discourse: "—She too wants me to catch hold of her, he thought. That's why she came with me to the tram. I could easily catch hold of her when she comes up to my step: nobody is looking. I could hold her and kiss her." The character's interior speech is utilized here as the equivalent of a stage monologue or aside in drama. It has the form of direct discourse but a different effect. In part 2, section 3, the narrator carries his modifications further during Stephen's encounter with his schoolmate Heron just before the play. We are given the narrative of Stephen's heretical essay and the drubbing it leads to as scene, dialogue, and action. But this narrative occurs in Stephen's mind. His memory now is rendered in nearly the same way as the narrator's presentation of the external world. The growing resemblance between the two modes of narration prepares for the more radical alignment of teller and character that occurs later.

The more striking fusion of inner and outer and of character and teller begins emerging in the next part, when the teller adopts the narrated monologue while presenting the retreat in part 3, section 2. As in the narration of the Christmas dinner, the telling alternates between an external scene (the sermons) and Stephen's reaction to the outer world. Although the narrator continues to employ techniques introduced in previous sections, there are some crucial modifications. These changes suggest, among other things, the intensity of Stephen's reaction to events. Section 2 consists of an introductory talk and three sermons that take place on consecutive days. The initial, prominent use of narrated monologue occurs in the passage presenting Stephen's walk home the first evening after the introductory talk: "So he had sunk to the state of a beast that licks his chaps after meat. This was the end; . . . And that was life." The device is especially manifest because Joyce uses demonstrative pronouns in a paragraph otherwise relatively free of them. The statements can be easily transformed into the character's speech to himself in first person and present tense. In the paragraph that follows, the narrator presents the initial sermon, on death and judgment in a curious way. He renders it not as direct discourse, the technique he uses to report the two subsequent sermons on hell, but as speech mediated by Stephen's consciousness. The brief passage of narrated monologue acts as the preparation for this odd filtering of Father Arnall's words through Stephen's mind. The narration of the sermon begins in the past tense with a series of verbs and phrases indicating Stephen's consciousness is being rendered: "stirring his soul," "fear," "terror," "into his soul," "he suffered," "he felt." In the middle of the sermon, although the dashes of direct discourse are absent, the past tense is replaced with a mixture of tenses, including present and future, much closer to the quotation of the later sermons as speech.

After this lengthy report of Stephen's consciousness during the first sermon, the alternation of passages focusing on psyche with those focusing on scene is again established, but now the narrated monologue has become a recurring feature of the narration. The narrator employs it briefly but regularly throughout the remainder of part 3. In part 3, section 3, Stephen's thoughts are quoted directly, once with a dash indicating direct discourse when he hears voices but at other times without the dash as apparently unmediated interior exclamations: "Confess! Confess!" While this last exclamation can be read as a direct presentation of Stephen's thought, the similar one, "For him! For him!" that occurs only a page earlier is an instance of narrated monologue. We read "For him" as "For *me*," understanding the third person as applying to the character.

With a device as problematic as narrated monologue, there will almost certainly be some disagreement among readers concerning the application of the term to specific passages. Whatever the differing judgments about the particular passages I have identified as narrated monologue, the general point concerning the sudden, recurring appearance of the technique in the narration is irrefragable: these numerous possible instances of narrated monologue grouped together in part 3 mark a significant shift in the style. The shift is increasingly toward renderings of Stephen's intensely felt thoughts that create an ambiguity concerning the relationship of the style to the character's language. In the two remaining parts the narrator freely employs in combination the various techniques he has used to present Stephen's mind. Once the reader has grown accustomed to the different modes for representing consciousness that have been introduced seriatim over the course of nearly 150 pages, the teller can rely on the reader's newly created capacity for responding to the salmagundi of techniques that will now be employed in the narration.

The narrator has been making a persona for the reader as well as for himself in his portrayal of Stephen. The reader has learned the conventions of the literary techniques that the author uses to compose his own self-representation as teller and to present Stephen's gradually developing sensibilities. Only after all the techniques have become thoroughly established as conventions of the fiction can the narrator begin to shift rapidly from one to another. The swift alternation of devices evoking the hard, gemlike flame of Stephen's mind occurs in the book's two climactic segments: at the end of part 4, section 3, when Stephen is on the strand, and during Stephen's composing of his villanelle in part 5. At the end of part 4, section 3, the narrator gives us Stephen's interior exclamations, "Yes! Yes! Yes!" combined with possible instances of narrated monologue and with Stephen's thoughts quoted as if they were direct discourse: "—Heavenly God! cried Stephen's soul, in an outburst of profane joy." Near the end of my discussion of *A Portrait,* I shall deal with the implications of the similar combination in part 5, section 2.

In part 5 there are numerous instances of narrated monologue. The narrator also employs at great length the technique he used in part 2, section 3, by presenting Stephen's memories while he is walking to the university as scene, action, and dialogue (as in the long recollection of Davin's story about his walk in the country and his encounter with the peasant woman.) The ambiguity about the source of the narration's language is particularly pronounced throughout part 5. Repeatedly the narrator introduces long passages of Stephen's thoughts by asserting first that Stephen "watched," "saw," "looked at," or "had heard" something, then that someone or something "seemed" a certain way. These passages omit the phrase "to him" or "to Stephen," which would identify explicitly the language to follow as Stephen's rather than the narrator's. The narrator will introduce a long paragraph of revery with only a brief reference to "Stephen's mind," which the reader may tend to forget, or he will conclude rather than introduce such a long paragraph with a phrase indicating the passage was Stephen's "thought." As in so many other late passages, the effect is to align the teller's voice and the character's, if only temporarily. The residual and cumulative sense of merger created by such alignments molds the reader's stance toward the narration with particular force. While *some* distinctions can be made between teller and character (this discussion would not have been possible without them), the passages ask us again and again to consider the relationship of the two voices that are so complexly mixed.

The subtly mingled but counterpointed language of teller and character emerges vividly in the book's second half, primarily because the narrated monologues together with the related techniques appear frequently beginning in part 3, section 2. Along with the seemingly intimate presentation of Stephen's thoughts, in part 5 the reader encounters longer and more elaborate statements to his companions than Stephen has made earlier. His voices, both internal and public, are thrust to the foreground. At the book's ending, it is primarily these voices that determine the reader's overall judgment of Stephen's potential.

JOURNAL AND EPIGRAPH: BEGINNING AND HOMEWARD GLANCE

The representations of Stephen's consciousness that occur in part 5 are particularly relevant for understanding the relationship of narrative to narration in *A Portrait*. The following paragraph, in which Stephen comments silently on Cranly's remark about a fellow student, is typical of the last section:

> It was his [Cranly's] epitaph for all dead friendships and
> Stephen wondered whether it would ever be spoken in the
> same tone over his memory. The heavy lumpish phrase
> sank slowly out of hearing like a stone through a quagmire.
> Stephen saw it sink as he had seen many another, feeling its
> heaviness depress his heart. Cranly's speech, unlike that of
> Davin, had neither rare phrases of Elizabethan English nor
> quaintly turned versions of Irish idioms. Its drawl was an
> echo of the quays of Dublin given back by a bleak decaying
> seaport, its energy an echo of the sacred eloquence of Dublin
> given back flatly by a Wicklow pulpit.

Such insertions, made by the narrator during his report of conversations, amount to brief digressions. As part of a commentary on time in fiction, Jean Ricardou remarks on the effect passages like this one can have in a narrative. Because of their length, they disrupt any illusion of a continuous flow of time in the plot by calling attention to the time of the narration. As Ricardou says, they emphasize "the writing (habitually concealed by the story)." When their prominence begins to define the mode of narration, as it does in *A Portrait,* in Ricardou's formulation the work "ceases to be the writing of a story to become the story of a writing." The passage emphasizes writing in two senses, as process of narration and as style of language. The teller's activity of narrating is emphasized in ways it cannot be through the quotation of dialogue. And attention is drawn to the specific kind of language employed, particularly in this passage, in which Stephen explicitly makes contrasts between various styles.

As narration, *A Portrait* includes all the styles mentioned in the paragraph and many more. They are the literary styles the character has heard or read (and sometimes spoken) and that the narrator has adopted in his written mimicry of the character's mind and the character's world. At times we understand them primarily as styles within the narrative; at other times, as styles of the narration. When the styles characterize Stephen's thoughts intimately presented, distinguishing narrative from narration is often no longer possible. At issue in such a passage is the question of the nature of narrative as mimetic or as diegetic, a question treated at length by Gérard Genette. ("Boundaries of Narrative," *New Literary History* 8 [Autumn 1976]). The narration of *A Portrait* supports Genette's conclusion that all narrative is essentially diegetic and that pure mimesis is not possible. The speaking voice of the discourse is always evident. Narration is never simply a purely transparent vehicle for narrative. The language of narration is opaque. We see *it* as well as the story communicated, just as Stephen sees the phrase Cranly speaks. Stephen understands the semantic meaning of Cranly's words and the implication of Cranly's style. And the reader understands the implications of the narration, including the recurring reports of Stephen's thoughts.

Through an energetic echo that gives back Stephen's eloquence, the narrator fuses inextricably with character. There is no means for disentangling Stephen's attitudes from the voice of the narrator who speaks them. The two voices are linked by the author's act of writing, a mediating process we become aware of through the style of narration but can never experience directly. We know the product and its implications but not the process itself. Instead, we experience the analogous mediating process of the act of reading, which aligns *our* activities of mind with those of character and teller. As Wayne Booth has said, "Any sustained inside view, of whatever depth, temporarily turns the character whose mind is shown into a narrator." The narrator's reiterated shifts between internal and external views make *A Portrait* a work about the transforming of a character into an artist in which style regularly turns the character into a teller. When the style includes narrated monologue, the reader shares the role of teller with the character by speaking the character's mind.

The final style adopted by the narrator, one especially pertinent to the present inquiry, is that of the journal, from which the entries of March 20 through April 27 are apparently only an excerpt. In the narrative's fictive chronology, as distinct from the chronology of narration, the journal is the last example of Stephen's styles as well. The potential ambiguity of the word "last" is the crux of the difference between the narrative and the narration. The style of the journal displaces the villanelle, the aesthetic theory, and the other examples of Stephen's expression—written, spoken, and internal—that are either directly presented or alluded to earlier. In its turn, the styles of the entire book displace that of the journal. The dual, interlocking process of feedback points to the problem of the ending and the end toward which the narrative tends. Two styles, the teller's and the character's, not just one, are brought to conclusion, or at least partial closure, in the one document that can be read as two documents. The journal kept by a character is also a portion of a narrative reported by the teller.

There is an acute disequilibrium between process and product, between Stephen's activity of keeping a journal and the portion excised by the narrator through an act of quotation that resembles the reporting of dialogue. The reader of *Ulysses* faces an analogous situation, for the language of "Penelope" presents two discourses simultaneously: the character's internal one, which is a process of mind, and the narrator's more public one, which is a style of language. The shifting focus becomes particularly evident for the reader of *A Portrait* who attempts to reconcile the journal in its fictional and textual contexts (of story and of narration) with the title and the epigraph of the title page and with the dates and places noted on the final page. All these parts of the book are relatively independent of what falls between them. Their implications do not appear at first to be wholly integrated with the remainder of the book as coherent aspects of style and story. This apparent failure of integration provides grounds for interpreting *A Portrait* as preposterous in that word's etymological sense.

Before and after, pre- and post-, are made to exchange places and to interact reciprocally. The exchange and interaction are manifest in the ending, from the perspective of which the reader revises the provisional interpretations generated up to that state of the reading. At the end of any narrative the reader engaged in an interpretive process experiences the preposterous aspect of reading. The reader's new perspective for scrutinizing the text's details allows a look backward that sees the text in retrospective arrangement. That arrangement modifies and displaces provisional readings, which are now seen anew in revision. The reading process flows temporally from the present to the past as the reader experiences portions of the text becoming parts of new contexts that are the bases for reinterpretations. Prospective and retrospective, provisional and revisionary judgments merge as the reader encounters and assimilates the conceptual implications of the narrative's form. The reader's experience of retrospective rearrangements shifting places through time duplicates the character's experience when he becomes the teller of his own tale in retrospect.

The closing of both book and journal with the notation of dates and places, "Dublin 1904 / Trieste 1914," presents in small the problematic, preposterous quality of the entire work. The reader must decide whether the references are part of the story or part of the writing, whether they are appropriate to the product or to the process of creation. Like the title, they refer at once to both product and process, to both character and author as artists. The autobiographical bases of the dates and places are well known. They point to the time and locations at which the author initiates and completes the writing of the book. Joyce finished *A Portrait* in Trieste just over ten years after leaving Dublin. Serial publication began in 1914. The authorial, autobiographical significance in no way diminishes the relevance the references possess for Stephen Dedalus's story. There is a complicated, uncanny doubling lurking within and behind the apparently innocent closing that is a *post scriptum*. This doubling that occurs through the telling of the story is more radical than most interpretations have allowed. Its precedent in Joyce's earlier fiction is found in "A Painful Case." In that story the central character, James Duffy, "had an odd autobiographical habit which led him to compose in his mind from time to time a short sentence about himself containing a subject in the third person and a predicate in the past tense" ("Dublin 1904 / Trieste 1914").

The strange duplication becomes apparent once dates and times are both understood as referring to Joyce's process of writing *and* to the story of Stephen Dedalus as it appears to develop beyond the time of the excerpt printed from the journal. Although no exact dates are ever provided for Stephen's activities earlier in the narrative, Dublin is obviously the place appropriate to the journal and to much of the action, and 1904 is within the limits of probability suggested in the fiction. Nineteen fourteen would be the year and Trieste the place in which Stephen completes the transforming of the journal into a book that is the simulacrum of Joyce's. The last portion of *A Portrait* presents what comes first with respect to the remainder of the text. In Stephen Dedalus's fictional life, which includes his life as a writer of fiction, the keeping of the journal precedes the completing of the book. The last—that is, the most recent—stage of Stephen's development as an artist is presented through the narration, not in the narrative. The dates and places that stand both inside and outside the story are the signatures of author and character as writers, their superimposed self-portraits painted in the corner of the finished canvas. They are the equivalent of the closing that Stanislaus Joyce reports his brother intended to append to *Stephen Hero,* "the signature, *Stephanus Daedalus Pinxit.*"

In Ovid's *Metamorphoses* the line quoted as epigraph to *A Portrait* refers to the mythic artist Daedalus, the "old father, old artificer" mentioned at the end of Stephen's journal. Ovid presents Daedalus setting his mind to work upon unknown arts. As with the notations at the book's end, the question of the epigraph's meaning concerns its referent. Like the journal, the epigraph is presented as a fragment quoted out of its original context. For the epigraph, but not for the journal, the original context is available to be examined. There is no evidence that the fragmentary journal actually has an origin in the same way as the epigraph does. In the *Metamorphoses* the epigraph's context indicates Daedalus's longing for home:

> Homesick for homeland, Daedalus hated Crete
> And his long exile there, but the sea held him.
> . . . He turned his thinking
> Toward unknown arts, changing the laws of nature.

In the case of Ovid's Daedalus, the act of turning the mind to work on obscure arts has an explicit cause and an explicit effect. Daedalus fashions wings for himself and for Icarus in order to escape from a prison and return home. Daedalus's work violates the laws of nature through the accomplishment of a feat seemingly beyond human possibility. The result also includes the death of Icarus, an apparently unavoidable concomitant of the mature artist's act of making in order to escape.

At the beginning of *A Portrait* as well as at its end, Joyce challenges the laws of conventional narrative by turning his own mind to intricate arts that result in a death and a doubling through the creation of a ghostly presence for the artist in a voice that repeats itself. Like the designations of place and time, the epigraph refers to the Dedalian character as well as to the Daedalian author. When the character's role as son is over after the final page, his fatherly role as teller is born phoenixlike to return home on the first page. Character transforms himself into artist as the son becomes his own father. Essential to the transformation is the importance of home in both Ovid's work and Joyce's. The act of producing the portrait combines the longing for home with the homecoming itself. *A Portrait* is the *nostos* whose end is continuous with its beginning, a beginning to which it returns the reader and the character in a way that anticipates the recirculating structure of *Finnegans Wake*.

As in *Ulysses* and *Finnegans Wake,* in *A Portrait* Joyce presents both fathers and sons in analogous relationships to mythic figures: HCE with Shem and Shaun, Ulysses with Telemachus, Daedalus with Icarus. The doubling in all these texts is accompanied by the unity of parent with child. Both roles are associated with a single character and with the special figure who tells the tale. According to one of the washerwomen in the ALP section of *Finnegans Wake,* "every telling has a taling and that's the he and the she of it." In the production of literary texts, the artist achieves a state comparable to androgyny, in which a procreative act occurs that results in the literary progeny. The washerwoman's later statement, "We'll meet again, we'll part once more," indicates the nature of the process and product of creation. Author and text are one in a unity in separation like that of parent and child or of husband and wife. This strange but familiar unity is reflected in the relationships of teller to character, teller to tale, and teller to reader in all Joyce's longer fiction. Such a unity finds an appropriate stylistic expression in the narrated monologue.

In *A Portrait* the mutually self-engendering relationships of teller to character come close to being explicitly presented. The author's persona as narrator tells the story of a young man developing into a writer. The journal Stephen Dedalus produces is part of the workshop from which issues the story of a young man developing into a writer, and so on. The nature of the journal in *A Portrait,* along with the elliptical letter in the *Wake,* suggests that the Möbius strip provides the nearest structural analogue for the relation of narrative to narration in Joyce's fiction after *Dubliners.* Because some of the large movements of Joyce's narratives are finite but unbounded, they are capable of a precise definition that is a description of the perpetual circulation called "continuarration" in *Finnegans Wake.* The recirculation can be described through Möbean geometry because father and son, teller and tale, teller and character are one. For Ovid, Daedalus and Icarus are separate. For Joyce they are not. Stephen as character and as narrator is both the immature and the mature artist, both Icarus and Daedalus. Because of the narrative's peculiar form, Stephen's destiny, like the fate of the mythic figures behind and within Joyce's fiction, is to be read as dual. According to Tiresias, Odysseus will return home but also continue wandering. In *Ulysses* Odysseus's double destiny is split between Stephen Dedalus and Leopold Bloom at the narrative's end when the former decides to wander and the latter chooses to remain at home. The two fates are combined for the narrator of *Ulysses,* whose stylistic divagations bring him home and redefine home.

In *A Portrait,* because Stephen exhibits the antithetical traits of Daedalus and Icarus in his two manifestations, the Daedalian narrator can present the young protagonist in the guise of an Icarus transforming himself into a Daedalus. Both Odysseus and Daedalus are homesick and homeward bound in their myths. At the end of *A Portrait* Stephen it outward bound, having determined to serve no longer. Stephen's decision to leave is necessarily connected for the reader to his act of keeping a journal, for the presentation of the journal signals Stephen's departure. But the keeping of the journal, which indicates the decision to write as well as to leave, is glossed by the epigraph. In order to write Stephen turns his mind to obscure arts, arts that lead him far from home, as Daedalus is led far from home, but these arts inevitably bring him back to a home, not literally but literarily. The subject of the journal that ostensibly announces departure from home, like the subject of the book containing the journal, is home, as well as the displacements of wandering. For Joyce, to turn the mind toward intricate arts is to look homeward. In the act of refusing to serve the home, the artist makes it possible for the home to serve him as the primary material for his art. Daedalus and Icarus, Sicily and Crete, Trieste and Dublin, 1914 and 1904, Stephen as teller and Stephen as character all merge in the book's oscillating focus. In *A Portrait* and later, the homeward look, no matter how intricately expressed in and as wanderings of style, involves a merging of citizen and artist that occurs in the encounters of reader and teller and of reader and character. In Joyce's fiction the two encounters are not necessarily distinct.

The language of the one book casts two shadows, projects two images related by superimposition as in a palimpsest. The character who tells his own tale never writes on a tabula rasa. He always and inevitably displaces the past by erasing it and writing over the erasure, even when the writing constitutes a recapturing of the past as well as a displacing of it. Like Tristram Shandy and every other teller, Stephen Dedalus as writer can never capture himself or his own process of writing. He can only suggest the nature of the activity of writing as self-portrayal, as self-representation. The pretext for the narration given in the title, to portray a young, developing artist, precedes the reader's experience of the story. But the prior text for the character, the writing that precedes the text temporally in the character's experience, is the journal that is part of the book as well as prior to it. That journal allows the reader to redefine the narrative in a new frame of reference. By experiencing the earlier text as both behind the later one and within it, the reader can see through, as well as by means of, the story's pretense.

Joyce's *Portrait* and the Proof of the Oracle

Patrick Parrinder

The Portrait and the Artist

The text of *A Portrait of the Artist as a Young Man* is dated "Dublin 1904 / Trieste 1914." The year 1904 was the year in which *Stephen Hero* was written and Joyce left Dublin with Nora Barnacle to become a language teacher on the Adriatic. Ten years later, after some vicissitudes, he was still there. His life was about to be transformed, thanks to the First World War (which would force him to move to neutral Switzerland), and to a chance letter from Ezra Pound in December 1913, which marked the beginnings of his literary celebrity. Pound arranged for serial publication of the *Portrait* to begin in the *Egoist,* a small avant-garde literary and political magazine, in February 1914; in June of the same year the London publisher Grant Richards at last brought out *Dubliners.*

The writing of the *Portrait* thus spans ten years during which Joyce kept rigorously to Stephen Dedalus's programme of "silence exile and cunning." His literary silence was broken only by *Chamber Music* and by a small quantity of essays and journalism, some of it written in Italian. His exile, at first only temporary, was confirmed by his unhappy experiences in revisiting Ireland in 1909 and 1912. Cunning is evident in the far-reaching revisions with which he transformed *Stephen Hero,* a raw apprentice-work, into the *Portrait* with its eloquence of style and fastidious pursuit of artistic imper-

From *James Joyce.* © 1984 by Cambridge University Press.

sonality. Joyce makes Stephen Dedalus echo the famous passage in Flaubert's *Letters* which declares that the writer should stand aloof from his work: "The artist must stand to his work as God to his creation, invisible and all powerful; he must be everywhere felt but nowhere seen." The *Portrait of the Artist* brings the doctrine of impersonality to bear in an area which Flaubert himself had never attempted. It sets out to be an impersonal or ironic autobiography.

The irony consists in Joyce's balancing of the different points of view it is possible to adopt towards the young Stephen. Stephen himself comes to believe he is following a predestined course, and unfolds a fervently idealistic artistic creed. Through him Joyce is able both to affirm the romantic myth of artistic genius, and to partially dissociate himself from the arrogance and self-conceit which follows from that myth. Irony is always implicit in the narrative, yet it cannot be too heavily underlined or it will destroy the basis of Joyce's—not merely Stephen's—claims for his writing. The book is uncertainly poised between mature reservation and an almost intoxicating sympathy with Stephen's experience. Finally, it may be, the artist-myth in the *Portrait* taken on its own was too powerful, and Joyce's attempt to relive it burst the bounds of mature detachment. He then had to create a disillusioned sequel to his autobiographical novel, in the parts of *Ulysses* centred on Stephen.

Joyce started off, as few if any novelists before him had done, by sticking scrupulously to the ostensible facts of his own life. His rewriting of the main events of his life is as nothing compared with the melodramatic inventions to be found in even the most "confessional" of earlier novels. This is the main point of difference between the *Portrait* and the *Bildungsromane* and *Künstlerromane* ("novels of education" and "artist-hero" novels) of the nineteenth century. The *Portrait* is less close to books like *Wilhelm Meister, David Copperfield,* or Gissing's *New Grub Street* than it is to the genre of literary autobiography and memoirs. The pattern of destiny which Stephen discovers in the events of his own life suggests that one crucial source is the tradition of spiritual apology or confession, from St Augustine to Newman. Stephen's destiny, however, bears witness to the religion of Art rather than of Christianity, and it is in the field of artistic memoirs and autobiographical sketches that we shall find the closest analogues to the *Portrait*. One such memoir by an older contemporary—George Moore's *Confessions of a Young Man* (1888)—no doubt influenced Joyce's title.

Stephen's belief in the priestly role of the artist and his duty to "forge in the smithy of my soul the uncreated conscience of my race" has its roots in the high romanticism of Wordsworth and Shelley. The *Portrait* transmutes the stuff of actual experience into artistic myth as thoroughly as Wordsworth had done. In addition, it serves as a "prelude" in the Wordsworthian sense to the more comprehensive edifices of *Ulysses* and *Finnegans Wake*. Nevertheless, the *Portrait* is not a straightforwardly romantic work. While Stephen remains ultimately committed to the Shelleyan notion of the artist as unacknowledged legislator of the world, his attention—unlike that of the Wordsworthian or Shelleyan hero—is devoted to disentangling himself from the external world and exploring the secrets and intricacies of his own art. His preoccupation with art as a sacred mystery links him to the Aesthetic and Decadent movements of the late nineteenth century. The reverence that the Aesthetes and Decadents felt for their romantic predecessors was tinged by the melancholy conviction that these poets had sought in the external world for "what is there in no satisfying measure or not at all." (These words, borrowed from Walter Pater, were used by Joyce himself in his essay on the Dublin romantic poet James Clarence Mangan.) The artist now turned, not to unspoilt nature, but in on himself to find a truly satisfying richness and beauty. Oscar Wilde went so far as to suggest that all artists are solipsists, whether they know it or not: "Every portrait that is painted with feeling is a portrait of the artist," we read in *The Picture of Dorian Gray*. It may have been a similar conviction that led Joyce to turn to autobiographical fiction in the first place.

Stephen Hero is written in the naturalistic manner and portrays Stephen, during his student years, as an Ibsenite. Early in 1904, however, Joyce had written a short essay called "A Portrait of the Artist" which contrasts sharply with *Stephen Hero* even though Joyce incorporated some passages from it into his novel. The "Portrait of the Artist" was—understandably—rejected by the editors of *Dana* as incomprehensible. Far from presenting the artist as a free-standing fictional character, through realistic description and dramatized dialogue, Joyce had written a tortuous, allusive and contemplative essay modelled on the Walter Pater of *Imaginary Portraits* (1887). Such a portrait was, as he expressed it, "not an identificative paper but rather the curve of an emotion." The artist portrayed is one who turns aside from his contemporaries to seek the "image of beauty" in the byways of esoteric and occult learning. Though the essay concludes with a Shelleyan vision of social revolution, there is no suggestion here (as there was in the "epiphany" passage in *Stephen Hero*) that the artist might find beauty in the "commonest object" or amongst the people around him. Instead, "to those multitudes not as yet in the wombs of humanity but surely engenderable there, he would give the word."

The artist, if he is to "give the word" to future humanity, must follow the image of beauty and free himself of all servitude to the words of those alien to him. That is equally the message of the 1904 "Portrait" and of its 1916 counterpart. In the mature *Portrait* the words of others are dramatized as external and internal voices. The book begins with the voice of Stephen's father and ends with Stephen's departure for the continent at the behest of imaginary voices clamouring; "We are your kinsmen." At this point he has rejected his father's voice in favour of voices he believes to be more "authentic," more "internal." They are at once the Sibylline voices of inspiration and prophecy and the voices of his fellow-artists in the literary tradition. Nevertheless, Stephen's ability to discover such authentic voices remains unproven, since only in his career as a writer, which he has yet to begin, can he break his self-imposed silence and show that he, too, has it in him to "give the word." The proof of the oracle would be found in the writing.

Voice, Memory, and Discontinuity

"The past assuredly implies a fluid succession of presents, the development of an entity of which our actual present is a phase only," Joyce had declared in his 1904 essay. The "actual presents" out of which his successive attempts at autobiographical fiction were written included, of necessity, a strong autobiographical urge. The same urge is present at least incipiently in every earlier stage of Stephen's childhood and youth. We see him not only learning about and reacting to his environment, but creating a sense of identity based on accumulated experience and feelings. His sense of identity is intimately connected with memory, and the *Portrait* begins, effectively, at the point where Stephen as an infant first exercises his powers as a memoirist. The description of him as "retaining nothing of all he read save that which seemed to him an echo or prophecy of his own state" belongs to a particular phase of adolescence, yet it is also deeply characteristic of Stephen from the beginning. His inner knowledge of his own identity is ratified by his discovery of a series of prophecies, signs of a predestined outcome to his story, of which the principal one is his own name. The oddity of the name Dedalus is foregrounded very early in the *Portrait:* eventually he realizes it is "a prophecy of the end he had been born to serve," in other words, of artisthood. Joyce uses the twin themes of predestination and habitual autobiography to persuade us of the inevitability of Stephen's emergence as a writer, a career towards which he is seen to be innately predisposed. And, as an embryo writer, he is ceaselessly rewriting the "book of himself" (*Ulysses*).

The narrative structure of the *Portrait* is a "fluid succession of presents" (though each present is narrated in the past tense) linked by an evolutionary process, which shows the development of Stephen's identity and his accumulated memory. Each phase in the "succession of presents" is a tightly constructed narrative unit which may seem sharply discontinuous with what comes before and after it. The discontinuity is textual and generic as well as temporal; in the *Portrait,* as in *Ulysses,* Joyce's method amounts to "one style per episode." Linking the episodes is a series of evolutionary chains of images and themes. It is helpful to enumerate these, and I shall do so in unsystematic fashion beginning with Stephen's understanding of his surname.

The epigraph of the *Portrait* is from Ovid and denotes the Dedalian theme: "And he sets his mind to work upon unknown arts" (*Et ignotas animum dimittit in artes*). Nasty Roche commences hostilities with his famous question to Stephen in the first Clongowes episode—"What kind of a name is that?" The oddity of his name is further noticed by Athy, and, much later, by Stephen's fellow-student Davin who asks whether it is Irish. Stephen's reply, offering to show Davin his family tree in the Office of Arms, is a brazen attempt by Joyce to naturalize the palpably fictional. Earlier we have listened to Stephen trying out his name as it would look if he joined the priesthood—"The Reverend Stephen Dedalus, S.J."—and finding it does not fit. His eventual discovery that the name Dedalus is emblematic of the artist, and that it betokens the artist's means of escape from the island of his birth and imprisonment, comes pat like the solution to a detective story which has been kept hidden by simply diverting the reader's attention.

Stephen's discovery of the significance of his name comes about as a result of his increasingly specialized involvement with language. The very first game that he plays is a language-game, in which he turns Dante's proverbial (and rhyming) threat about eagles into a symmetrical pair of verses:

> Pull out his eyes,
> Apologise,
> Apologise,
> Pull out his eyes.

At Clongowes, the formal process of learning has begun and Stephen spontaneously extends this to learning about language. He is fascinated by the different meanings of such "queer words" as "belt" and "suck," as well as by the correspondence between words and things which allows cold and hot water to come out of taps marked cold and hot. In adolescence the secrets of his awakening sexuality and of his difference from his father are summed up in the shock of the word "Foetus" scratched on a desk. In the recognition scene on Dollymount beach there is a famous (if slightly obscure) passage in which Stephen becomes conscious of his obsession with words:

> He drew forth a phrase from his treasure and spoke it softly to himself:
> —A day of dappled seaborne clouds.
> The phrase and the day and the scene harmonised in a chord. Words. Was it their colours? He allowed them to glow and fade, hue after hue: sunrise gold, the russet and green of apple orchards, azure of waves, the greyfringed fleece of clouds. No, it was not their colours: it was the poise and balance of the period itself. Did he then love the rhythmic rise and fall of words better than their associations of legend and colour? Or was it that, being as weak of sight as he was shy of mind, he drew less pleasure from the reflection of the glowing sensible world through the prism of a language manycoloured and richly storied than from the contemplation of an inner world of individual emotions mirrored perfectly in a lucid supple periodic prose?

The passage is at once argument and evocation. To the extent that it presents genuinely alternative views of language, they are the major doctrines held by nineteenth- and early twentieth-century romantic poets, spelt out one by one. Stephen appears to be rejecting Keatsian verbal associationism, "Pure Sound" and Paterian or Conradian impressionism in favour of an expressionist model of language as the precise representation of an "inner world" of individual emotions, a view which should have found favour with T. S. Eliot. Language, moulded by the genius of the artist, has then become a "perfect mirror." If this is the ideal toward which the young Stephen aspires, the fifth section of the *Portrait* suggests the sort of resistance in language he may be destined to encounter. For Stephen is a poet, the author of a villanelle full of "coloured" words, and not yet capable of "lucid supple periodic prose" such as we find in *Dubliners*. Moreover, the vocabulary which surrounds him is not individual or authentic but secondhand. Debating the word "tundish" with the dean of studies, he reflects:

> How different are the words *home, Christ, ale, master,* on his lips and on mine! I cannot speak or write these words without unrest of spirit. His language, so familiar and so foreign, will always be for me an acquired speech. I have not made or accepted its words. My voice holds them at bay. My soul frets in the shadow of his language.

Stephen in the *Portrait* is searching for an authentic language which he can voice. It is a typically romantic quest, inherited by the symbolists and Decadents of the late nineteenth century and passed on to the early modernists. Arthur Symons's words in the peroration to *The Symbolist Movement in Literature* (1899) are representative:

> Here, then, in this revolt against exteriority, against rhetoric, against a materialistic tradition; in this endeavour to disengage the ultimate essence, the soul, of whatever exists and can be realised by the consciousness; in this dutiful waiting upon every symbol by which the soul of things can be made visible; literature, bowed down by so many burdens, may at last attain liberty, and its authentic speech.

Stephen, as poet and aesthetic theorist, should have been in full agreement with Symons's exhortation. Symons's vocabulary is close to the *Portrait* and, moreover, he had dedicated his book to Yeats, whose verses from *The Countess Cathleen* are echoed by Stephen. But that is not the whole story. It is fairly clear what direction a young Irish romantic, attracted by the Decadence and chafing against the "acquired speech" of his British rulers, might have been expected to take around 1900. Among the leaders of the 1916 Easter Rising were at least two published poets, Pearse and MacDonagh. It is the Irish nationalist in Stephen which makes him reflect, of *home, Christ, ale* and *master,* that "I cannot speak or write these words without unrest of spirit." Yet he is too honest to suppose that Gaelic, for him, would be any less of an acquired and secondhand speech. As he became an international writer Joyce tended more and more to represent the state of not being at home in one's language as a universal condition, the fate of fallen man after Babel rather than a product of the power-structure of the British Empire. In *Finnegans Wake* there is no "authentic speech," since everything comes at secondhand; the "voices" Joyce creates emerge from his mental "word-processor" and are in no sense prior to, or more authentic than, the actual writing. In the *Portrait* there are one or two anticipations of Joyce's later comic sense of the use, and inevitability, of borrowed speech. Stephen takes over words and phrases of the Elizabethans, for example, to serve as an erotic shorthand. Cranly's absurd dog-Latin does a good deal to enliven the dialogues of the final section. Joyce's later work implies that all modern literary language is bastardized and cut adrift from its roots—that language, in fact, has become grotesque. The world thus demands an art which reconciles Stephen's quest for a unique language with Cranly's ebullient philistinism.

Two further developing themes in the *Portrait* have already been mentioned: voices and memory. To see how words, voice and memory are intertwined we need only consider the cry which issues from Stephen's lips as, possessed by the demon of lust, he wanders into the red-light district of Dublin for the first time:

> It broke from him like a wail of despair from a hell of sufferers and died in a wail of furious entreaty, a cry for an iniquitous abandonment, a cry which was but the echo of an obscene scrawl which he had read on the oozing wall of a urinal.

Words inscribed on a urinal wall (comparable, no doubt, to the word *"Foetus"* scratched on a desk) and then imprinted on his memory are "echoed" in a cry. Stephen's whole development could be expressed in terms of a vocal metabolism in which words and voices enter into his consciousness and are digested by the memory, before issuing forth as emotional statements of which the simplest form is the cry. The disjunction between outer and inner, between voices and cries, becomes obvious to Stephen in adolescence, when he feels it at first as a sickness interrupting normal digestion:

> His very brain was sick and powerless. He could scarcely interpret the letters of the signboards of the shops. By his monstrous way of life he seemed to have put himself beyond the limits of reality. Nothing moved him or spoke to him from the real world unless he heard in it an echo of the infuriated cries within him. He could respond to no earthly or human appeal, dumb and insensible to the call of summer and gladness and companionship, wearied and dejected by his father's voice.

Though it may weary him at this moment, his father's voice plays a crucial part in the novel. The *Portrait* begins (as we have seen) with his father's words and ends with a cry addressed to an imaginary father. Stephen's father's voice triumphs over Dante's voice in the Christmas dinner scene, though both are etched into the young boy's consciousness. When in adolescence he wearies of his actual father's voice, he is all the more vulnerable to those of the "spiritual fathers," the priests. Joyce, indeed, introduces a startling innovation which amounts to a scandalous breach of the rules of modern fictional construction. In the third chapter the priest's voice takes over and dominates the *Portrait,* through the series of sermons which occupies nearly thirty pages of text or almost one-eighth of the whole book.

After the priest's voice, it is the turn of the voices of nature and the imagination, which Stephen hears on the beach as he decides that his destiny is to be an artist. Once that decision is made he is again haunted by the voices of his social environment, which are raised against him in reproach. Leaving his house on the way to the university, he hears the screech of a mad nun but "shook the sound out of his ears by an angry toss of his head":

> His father's whistle, his mother's mutterings, the screech of an unseen maniac were to him now so many voices offending and threatening to humble the pride of his youth.

Stephen "drove their echoes even out of his heart with an execration," but they are not to be dismissed so easily. Davin puts the
claims of nationality, language and religion to him. His mother's
voice is emphasized towards the end of the novel, pleading with him
not to desert his religion and praying, Stephen reports, "that I may
learn in my own life and away from home and friends what the heart
is and what it feels." Nevertheless, he can summon up imaginary
voices which assure him he is right. Just before his final walk with
Cranly he gains strength in his fight with his mother from the cries
of swallows returning from migration. "The inhuman clamour
soothed his ears in which his mother's sobs and reproaches mur-
mured insistently"; the birds, as Stephen tells himself by means of
pedantic references to Swedenborg and Cornelius Agrippa, are
age-old vehicles of augury. The final picture of Stephen is of one
who is stubborn enough, by and large, to make the voices around
him tell him what he wants to hear. But it is not always so, and in
Ulysses the circumstances surrounding his mother's death will stretch
his ability to rationalize the path he has taken to the utmost.

The role of memory in the *Portrait* has already been touched
upon. Unlike most protagonists in autobiography, Stephen's memory is active and is foregrounded even in childhood. In one respect
this may seem no more than a compositional strategy: Stephen's first
days at Clongowes are not narrated chronologically but by means of
a series of flashbacks which betray the onset of fever, preventing him
from routine absorption in such activities as the game of football.
The term "flashback" suggests an automatic process, like that which
goes on in the cutting-room of a film studio. But Stephen's memory
is not only episodic and repetitive but creative. For example, the
train of references to the "square ditch" with its rats and cold slimy
water in the first few pages helps to determine the kind of person
Stephen becomes. Wells's action in shouldering him into the ditch is
probably the cause of his lifelong aquaphobia, seen in the beach
episode ("how his flesh dreaded the cold infrahuman odour of the
sea") and again in *Ulysses*. Memories of water at Clongowes—the
ditch, the turf-coloured bathwater, the "wettish" air—are so indel-
ible that they can eventually be classed as instinctual and shown to
influence the crucial decisions of his life. When Stephen is tempted to
join the priesthood, memories of Clongowes cause his soul to revolt
at the thought of collegiate life:

> He wondered how he would pass the first night in the
> novitiate and with what dismay he would wake the first
> morning in the dormitory. The troubling odour of the
> long corridors of Clongowes came back to him and he
> heard the discreet murmur of the burning gasflames. At
> once from every part of his being unrest began to irradiate.
> A feverish quickening of his pulses followed and a din of
> meaningless words drove his reasoned thoughts hither and
> thither confusedly. His lungs dilated and sank as if he were
> inhaling a warm moist unsustaining air and he smelt again
> the warm moist air which hung in the bath in Clongowes
> above the sluggish turfcoloured water.
>
> Some instinct, waking at these memories, stronger than
> education or piety, quickened within him at every near
> approach to that life, an instinct subtle and hostile, and
> armed him against acquiescence.

Its reliance on "instinct" rather than reason makes this a remarkably
original passage. Any nineteenth-century novelist could have shown
Stephen arguing with himself over the pros and cons of the priestly
life, but Joyce does not do this. The question is settled at a level of
feeling "stronger than education or piety" and therefore prior to
argument. Indeed, Stephen's decision is a bodily as much as a mental
event. He is not conscious at this moment of the alternatives to a
career in the Church; he is not yet ready to devote himself to art or
to opt to go to university. He rejects the priesthood not because he
wants to do something else, but because he knows he *is* something
else; and that is the sum of his accumulated and remembered
experiences which "quickens" within him as if it were life itself.
Towards the end of the *Portrait* the workings of Stephen's memory
begin to be overshadowed by his maturing intellect and imagination.
To trace the growth of intellect, imagination and memory together
would be to describe the *Portrait of the Artist* as a whole.

The *Portrait* is unified not only by the workings of its protagonist's memory, but by an "unconscious" textual memory or series of
repetitions, which are most easily traced at the level of imagery. Hugh
Kenner, in a 1948 article, pointed out that in the *Portrait* "the first two
pages, terminated by a row of asterisks, enact the entire action in
microcosm" ("The Portrait in Perspective," in *James Joyce: Two Decades of Criticism,* 2d ed.). From the first two pages we can trace

"verbal leitmotivs" or image-sets which recur throughout the narrative. Stephen's impressions in infancy can be broken down (with some complications) into a series of binary oppositions. Thematically the most important of these may be tabulated as follows:

father	mother
father and mother	baby
his father and mother	Eileen's father and mother
telling stories	playing the piano
storytelling and playing the piano	singing and dancing
the Michael Davitt brush (maroon)	the Parnell brush (green)
Dante's rewards (the cachous)	Dante's punishments (the eagles)

In addition to these thematic oppositions, there are others which seem purely imagistic:

wild rose blossoms	*green wothe botheth*
warm urine	cold urine
hiding under the table	the coming of the eagles
living next door to the Vances	

It is open to any reader to trace these oppositions through the book. Stephen's class at Clongowes is divided into rival teams, York and Lancaster (the white rose and the red rose). He reflects that you "could not have a green rose. But perhaps somewhere in the world you could." Maroon and green are the colours of Davitt and Parnell, so that the red and green of Christmas (holly and ivy, or the "great fire, banked high and red" and the ivy) betoken a political schism. When Stephen becomes pious, the rosaries he says "transformed themselves into coronals of flowers of such vague unearthly texture that they seemed to him as hueless and odourless as they were nameless." The blankness and inanition of the religious life, "a heart of white rose," is then contrasted with the red rose of passion and art, embodied both in the lotus-like apparition Stephen sees at the end of the beach episode and in the "roselike glow" he senses as he writes his villanelle. The lotus speaks to him of "some new world, fantastic, dim, uncertain as under sea, traversed by cloudy shapes and beings. A world, a glimmer, or a flower?" Yet Stephen's imaginary green rose retains a recognizable connection with Ireland and Parnell.

The one place where you could have a green rose is, of course, in the *Portrait of the Artist*.

Image-analysis of this sort will take us some way (though certainly not all the way) into Joyce's novel. It is not always clear that he exerts a very precise control over his images—often the repetitions elude any unforced critical explanation by their very frequency and diversity. For example, the Dedalian leitmotiv of flight is represented by various images of birds and bats that crop up in Stephen's consciousness. Plainly his interest in flight connects with his fear of water (aquaphobia). During his adolescent religious phase he feels himself "standing far away from the flood [of sexual desire] on a dry shore." Stephen is not deeply attracted by the dryness of asceticism as manifested in the "pale loveless eyes" of the Jesuit priest; he wants to feel superior to the element of water, rather than just safely dryshod. Images of birds abound in the *Portrait,* but it is only in the beach scene and the scene on the steps of the National Library that the bird-images appear portentous or symbolic. The ancient hero whom Stephen adopts as his spiritual father is a "hawklike man flying sunward above the sea," and the cry that rises to Stephen's lips in this moment is the "cry of a hawk or eagle on high." Girls and women, also, are compared to flying creatures. Stephen's girl on the beach "seemed like one whom magic had changed into the likeness of a strange and beautiful seabird." Emma's life, he thinks, might be "simple and strange as a bird's life." The birdlike girl is thus a transfigured version of the shadowy Emma, Stephen's "beloved," but in the final chapter there is added a rather different, though equally idealized image of womanhood. Davin, the clean-limbed Irish nationalist and Gaelic sports enthusiast, tells Stephen of the pregnant countrywoman who invited him to her bed. To Stephen such guileless sexuality stands for the awakening soul of Ireland, "a type of her race and his own, a batlike soul waking to the consciousness of itself in darkness and secrecy and loneliness." (Why batlike? Presumably because bats are the quietest and most furtive of flying creatures.) The batlike soul is an image of much more than merely sexual promise; indeed it is as it were abstracted from sex. Davin's woman is made to stand for Stephen's potential audience, the type of person for whom he is to go out and "forge in the smithy of my soul the uncreated conscience of my race."

The danger of the symbolic or imagistic reading of the *Portrait* is that it overlooks, of necessity, the discontinuities, shifts of perspective and changes of focus which fissure the narrative. When Mr Dedalus describes the betrayers of Parnell as "rats in a sewer," the alert symbolic reader will recall the rat that Stephen saw at Clongowes, and point to Stephen's identification with the victimized Irish leader. What we are witnessing, however, is a type of linguistic accident or coincidence in which the same semantic material has, in its new (and metaphorical) context, an utterly different value. Joyce himself was to become fascinated by such coincidences, but there is no sign that he gave deliberate attention to this particular example. The result of pursuing such chains of poetic association too far is to produce a *Portrait* very different from the one Joyce actually wrote.

The book is divided into five chapters, which exhibit a clear chronological, aetiological and stylistic progression. At the same time, each chapter roughly exhibits the same pattern of development. According to Kenner, the pattern is one of "dream nourished in contempt of reality, put into practice, and dashed by reality" ("The Portrait in Perspective"). Kenner describes the movement of the *Portrait* as a sort of vicious spiral, since "each chapter closes with a synthesis of triumph which in turn feeds the sausage-machine set up in the next chapter." The "synthesis of triumph," we might add, is in each case an approximation to the cry Stephen finally utters at the end of the book: "Welcome, O life!" Near the end of chapter 4 he exclaims, "To live, to err, to fall, to triumph, to recreate life out of life!" Chapter 3 ends with "Another life! A life of grace and virtue and happiness!"; chapter 2 with Stephen's first kiss which is a new awakening and an image of life; and chapter 1 with his successful appeal against injustice which leaves him feeling "happy and free" and hearing the sound of cricket bats "like drops of water in a fountain falling softly in the brimming bowl"—an image of plenty which is reminiscent of the Psalmist's "My cup runneth over." When Stephen at the end of the book announces that he is going "to encounter for the millionth time the reality of experience," it is (the structure implies) already the fifth in an exhilarating sequence of new starts.

This repeated rhythm in the *Portrait* should not, however, be allowed to obscure the sense of disjointedness that the book conveys, especially on close reading. The surviving portion of *Stephen Hero* presents a much more conventional, continuous progression than the finished version, which moves by leaps and jerks. It would be naive to pretend that Joyce's artistic control, as he revised his manuscript, was total or that the end-product is altogether seamless. Stephen's younger brother Maurice, an important character in the earlier version, has been eliminated from the *Portrait*—except that he does make a single unexplained appearance in chapter 2. ("—O, Holy Paul, I forgot about Maurice, said Mr Dedalus"—words which Joyce might have echoed.) When we read at the beginning of the Cork episode that "Stephen was once again seated beside his father in the corner of a railway carriage at Kingsbridge," and a moment later find him recalling "his childish wonder of years before and every event of his first day at Clongowes," it is not difficult to make out that Stephen's parents took him to Clongowes by train. The momentary flashback must refer to an earlier version of the *Portrait* which—as Joyce told his brother on December 15, 1907—"began at a railway station like most college stories." Joyce left traces of this beginning only in Stephen's memory—or did he, rather, forget to remove them?

The effect of the *Portrait*'s many narrative suppressions is not only to highlight the faculty of memory but to produce a book that has to be negotiated warily. When Stephen felt sick and feverish in the refectory at Clongowes,

> he leaned his elbows on the table and shut and opened the flaps of his ears. Then he heard the noise of the refectory every time he opened the flaps of his ears. It made a roar like a train at night. And when he closed the flaps the roar was shut off like a train going into a tunnel. That night at Dalkey the train had roared like that and then, when it went into the tunnel, the roar stopped. He closed his eyes and the train went on, roaring and then stopping; roaring again, stopping.

This passage once again feeds speculation about Stephen's first train journey, the source of the "childish wonder" he will eventually recall. Later that evening he imagines going home for the holidays in a "long long chocolate train with cream facings"—an amusing phrase in its own right, but also one which supports the conclusion that he went to Clongowes by train. Here, however, we have an evening journey passing through Dalkey on the line from Bray (where the Dedalus family lives) to Dublin. A few pages later we see Stephen again remembering the tunnel, and at the same time learning to manipulate metaphor:

> First came the vacation and then the next term and then
> vacation again and then again another term and then again
> the vacation. It was like a train going in and out of tunnels
> and that was like the noise of the boys eating in the
> refectory when you opened and closed the flaps of the ears.
> Term, vacation; tunnel, out; noise, stop.

This charming passage shows Stephen learning to understand his
experience, by reducing it to a kind of imaginative order. The in and
out of the tunnel, however, may serve as a metaphor for further
alternations in the opening chapter, which Stephen cannot perceive;
these are the alternations of narrative genre and of narrative units.
The first two pages of infantile consciousness have a poetic, not a
chronological form. (Chronologically they have no beginning or
end, though there could be no stronger poetic beginning than "Once
upon a time.") They give the effect of memories reassembled at a
later date. The first Clongowes episode, however, shows Stephen
actively using his imagination and memory, cut off as he is by fever
from unreflecting participation in the life around him. This abruptly
gives way to the Christmas dinner scene, a dramatized episode in
which Stephen's time for reflection is reduced to a minimum. The
second Clongowes episode is balanced between external event and
inner reflection. Stephen, having broken his glasses, is set somewhat
apart, though not as severely as when he was ill. His sensations of
pain and fear as the pandybat hits him are described with extraordinary vividness. His inner consciousness remains paramount as he
nerves himself up to complain to the rector, and walks alone through
the "low dark narrow corridor" not unlike a tunnel. Strengthened by
the legend of the Irish patriot Hamilton Rowan (who outwitted his
pursuers in the same place), Stephen emerges from this narrative
tunnel into the lucidity of his interview with the rector. These four
discontinuous episodes make up chapter 1 of the *Portrait*. Joyce's
suppression of linking passages in the narrative has become commonplace in twentieth-century fictional technique, though it was not
so when he was writing. The result is a compromise between the
linked collection of impressionistic stories or sketches (such as the
first three stories in *Dubliners*) and the discursive continuity of the
nineteenth-century novel.

    As we read on in the *Portrait* there are further marked disconti-
nuities. The sermons in the third chapter, the extended rhapsody on

the beach in the fourth, and the aesthetic dialogues and journal entries of the fifth are all an affront to conventional narrative decorum. Thanks to Joyce's extensive use of free indirect style, the book's vocabulary, syntax and cadence tend to become more complex as Stephen grows older. The *Portrait* for this reason is not a "well-made" novel in the nineteenth-century or the Jamesian sense, though it has often been acclaimed as an example, in Mark Schorer's phrase, of "technique as discovery." The changes in technique reflect the stages in Stephen's mental evolution, the growth of his soul. Alternatively, we may wish to see the discontinuities of the *Portrait* as an index of the changing pattern of voices surrounding and defining Stephen.

PHASES OF AN IDENTITY

Who is "Stephen"? The earliest episodes of the *Portrait* show him learning the identity that is given him by family and school. In each case, there are indications of a primal unity which has already given place to division. Soon, with the repercussions of Parnell's fall, the larger divisions of church and state will forcibly enter his own history.

When in the fifth chapter Cranly tries to persuade Stephen to make his Easter duty, he tells him that "whatever else is unsure in this stinking dunghill of a world a mother's love is not." Stephen first knows his mother as someone with a nice smell, who plays the piano so that he can dance. Yet even in the brief opening section she is present at a mysterious incident when he has done something wrong, and is required to apologize. Why did he hide under the table? Was it perhaps because he had expressed a wish to marry Eileen, the next-door girl whose family were Protestants? We do not know, but we do know that Stephen is conscious of estrangement from his mother very soon after this, as a result of being sent to boarding school. (Would Cranly have been so certain of a mother's love if *he* had been sent to boarding school?) The *Portrait* ends with Stephen saying goodbye to his mother and getting good advice from her; but the same thing also happens very close to the beginning. Even as a small child he has learnt the importance of a stiff upper lip on these occasions—"he had pretended not to see that she was going to cry. She was a nice mother but she was not so nice when she cried." That Stephen is adaptable enough to think of Clongowes as

his home is emphasized by the deeply satisfying entry on the flyleaf
of his geography book:

> Stephen Dedalus
> Class of Elements
> Clongowes Wood College
> Sallins
> County Kildare
> Ireland
> Europe
> The World
> The Universe

This is followed by a verse written by his schoolfellow Fleming "for
a cod":

> Stephen Dedalus is my name,
> Ireland is my nation,
> Clongowes is my dwellingplace
> And heaven my expectation.

Clongowes, unfortunately, is not the cosy place in a unified world
that these inscriptions describe. Rody Kickham, the boy's-school-
story hero, ignores Stephen; Wells and Nasty Roche subject him to
unpleasant inquisitions; and Wells has impulsively shouldered him
into the ditch. Wells wants to know if he kisses his mother, while
Roche tries to convict him of social inferiority by asking who his
father is. The other boys' fathers, or some of them, are country
gentry and magistrates; Mr Dedalus's decision to send his son to
Clongowes, however, is an act of social pretension he will be unable
to maintain for long. When Stephen, in the sick bay, fantasizes about
going home for Christmas, one of his most telling pieces of
wish-fulfilment is that "his father was a marshal now: higher than a
magistrate." Stephen wants to go one better than the other boys, not
merely to be like them. The only "marshal" he has encountered is a
former inhabitant of the house at Clongowes, whose ghost still
haunts the stairs. Soon Stephen is feeling sorry for his father, pitying
him for not having reached the magistracy. He remembers his
father's reasons for sending him to Clongowes—"his father had told
him that he would be no stranger there because his grand-uncle had
presented an address to the liberator there fifty years before"—and

perhaps dimly recognizes his family's doomed attempt to l[
past glories.

In dreaming that his father had become a marshal, Stephen is beginning that quest for a new and better father that will culminate in the *Portrait* in his idolization of the Greek hero Daedalus—though Daedalus in turn will be discarded, and Stephen will continue his quest for a spiritual father in *Ulysses*. Stephen's search originates as a psychic manifestation of the kind which Freud termed a "family romance." In a family romance, Freud wrote, "the child's imagination becomes engaged in the task of getting free from the parents, of whom he has a low opinion, and of replacing them by others who, as a rule, are of higher social standing" ("Family Romances," in *On Sexuality*). Stephen's family romance begins with the fantasy that his father's social standing has miraculously risen. Later he will come to the point of mentally disowning his family altogether: "He felt that he was hardly of the one blood with them but stood to them rather in the mystical kinship of fosterage, fosterchild and fosterbrother." In an extended sense, the family romance with its burden of fantasy-compensation for the inadequacies of the actual family is a pervading theme throughout Joyce's later work.

At home for Christmas, Stephen has been promoted from the nursery to the dignity of the family dining-table for the first time. The famous Christmas-dinner scene shows all pretence of family unity being shattered and, with it, Stephen's trust and confidence in his parents. The fall of Parnell, the Irish parliamentary leader, after the O'Shea divorce case in 1890 would have had legendary status in Irish history had Joyce never written; but the *Portrait* is a powerful addition to the legend. Stephen is "for Ireland and Parnell and so was his father." Parnell's fall coincides with a reversal in Simon Dedalus's fortunes, just as it did in the case of Joyce's own father. Simon invokes the authority of his ancestors, including a grandfather who was condemned to death as a "whiteboy" or rural insurrectionary; all these men, he claims, would have supported Parnell against the treacherous priests. The Catholic priests have betrayed Ireland before, reneging on Irish independence soon after the British government had passed the Catholic Emancipation Act of 1829. Simon encourages the blasphemies of his friend Mr Casey and declares that "we are an unfortunate priestridden race and always were and always will be till the end of the chapter." His attitude scandalizes Dante Riordan and opens a bitter conflict between the "patriarchy" and the "matriarchy" in Stephen's family.

The Christmas dinner is a powerfully dramatized episode in which we only intermittently share Stephen's thoughts. It is a miniature tragedy, carefully orchestrated by Joyce to include echoes of both Ibsen and Aristotle. At the end Mrs Riordan sweeps out, slamming the door and leaving the menfolk prostrated behind her rather like Nora Helmer in *A Doll's House*. Then there is an Aristotelian catharsis of pity and fear as Stephen raises his "terror-stricken face" and sees that "his father's eyes were full of tears." We must assume that the revolt of Dante, and his mother's ineffectual attempts as a peacemaker, leave Stephen's sympathies torn in two. He knows Mrs Riordan was a Parnellite until recently. Simon moreover, is clearly to blame for letting the quarrel get out of hand and spoil the Christmas dinner. Stephen is shocked by his father's coarse and self-indulgent anticlerical outburst—after all, it is his father who has sent him to Clongowes, to be taught by the priests. Though he recognizes that Parnell is the victim of injustice, Stephen cannot yet understand how injustice can be laid at the door of the Church. However, the next episode, in which he is brutally punished by Father Dolan for accidentally breaking his glasses, will speed up his education a little on this point.

The final Clongowes section replaces political and family trag-edy with a tragicomic episode which might have been modelled on the plot of the conventional boarding-school story. The episode begins and ends with the "pick, pack, pock, puck" of ball on cricket bat, and within it we hear another all-too-familiar sound, that of corporal punishment. It is a measure of the extent to which both his father and the priests have fallen in his eyes that, by the end of this section, Stephen has become his own romantic hero. He is egged on by the indignant and mutinous voices of his schoolmates, but, in deciding to complain to the rector about his unjust punishment, he is essentially on his own. His imagination calls up a whole series of mentors and father figures to sustain him in his resolve. Why did the prefect of studies have to ask twice what his name was? "The great men in history had names like that and nobody made fun of them." As he passes along the deserted corridor leading to the rector's room he is aware of the ghosts of the Jesuit saints, of the old marshal and of the patriot Hamilton Rowan (1751–1834), who escaped from the redcoats in this very house. Rowan and the marshal make an implicit link between the great men of history and the patriarchal tradition of the Dedalus family; we remember the grand-uncle who presented an address to the liberator (Daniel O'Connell, the hero of Catholic Emancipation) at Clongowes. History repeats itself, on a miniature scale. "The senate and the Roman people declared that Dedalus had been wrongly punished," as another boy puts it. As he comes back from the rector's office he is cheered by his schoolmates in triumph. His naive trust in family and school have been shaken, but he has learnt to believe in himself and has discovered, in the rector's magnanimity, a confirmation of the government of human life by an impartial court of appeal.

Stephen, however, is taken away from Clongowes, as his father cannot afford the fees. At the beginning of the second chapter he is back in the patriarchal world in which Uncle Charles and his father rehearse the family legends. Feminine influence on Stephen seems to have departed once Mrs Riordan abandoned the Christmas dinner-table and swept out of the door. His mother means little to Stephen and we see him as segregated from women, whether on his days with Uncle Charles, at his new school, Belvedere College (where boys take the female parts in the school play), or on his visit with his father to Cork. However, the male mentors who dominate this chapter come to seem both inadequate and fraudulent. Uncle Charles grows senile, Vincent Heron (Stephen's friend and rival at Belvedere) bullies him, and the rector of Clongowes comes down to earth so far as to share a joke with Simon about his son's pandying. Stephen finds himself beset by the pious exhortations and badgerings of male voices:

> While his mind had been pursuing its intangible phantoms and turning in irresolution from such pursuit he had heard about him the constant voices of his father and of his masters, urging him to be a gentleman above all things and urging him to be a good catholic above all things. These voices had now come to be hollowsounding in his ears. When the gymnasium had been opened he had heard another voice urging him to be strong and manly and healthy and when the movement towards national revival had begun to be felt in the college yet another voice had bidden him be true to his country and help to raise up her fallen language and tradition. In the profane world, as he

> foresaw, a worldly voice would bid him raise up his
> father's fallen state by his labours and, meanwhile, the
> voice of his school comrades urged him to be a decent
> fellow, to shield others from blame or to beg them off and
> to do his best to get free days for the school. And it was the
> din of all these hollowsounding voices that made him halt
> irresolutely in the pursuit of phantoms.

The "phantoms" that beckon Stephen to turn aside from the male world are, increasingly, those of real and imaginary women. Throughout the chapter Stephen is beset by sex. "He wanted to meet in the real world the unsubstantial image which his soul so constantly beheld." The unsubstantial image is represented by Mercedes, the heroine of *The Count of Monte Cristo,* and Stephen's attempts to locate the image in the real world are seen in his two failed trysts with a girl of his own age called Emma, and later in his visit to a prostitute. The chapter balances the growth of imagination against the moral squalor Stephen detects in his family now that his father's fortunes are in decline. Simon's hypocrisy, which is extravagantly displayed on the visit to Cork to sell off his property there, destroys any remaining illusions Stephen has about his family and its traditions.

The property in Cork, which Simon has squandered in his attempts to keep up the family appearances, should have been Stephen's inheritance. Throughout the visit Simon superbly patronizes his son, as if he were indeed coming into an inheritance rather than being done out of one. Stephen needs all the detachment and bitter aloofness he can muster to cope with his father's incessant cock-and-bantam rivalry. A tongue-tied silence characterizes much of his behaviour on the visit to Cork—an episode of interminable paternal monologues to which he listens without sympathy. In what one critic has called an "autobiography within an autobiography," Simon is telling his son the story of his life and covering up present failure with nostalgia for his cavalier youth. But for Stephen his torrent of self-indulgence is overshadowed by a single word cut on a desk in Queen's College—the word *"Foetus,"* which seems to express all the "monstrous reveries" and "monstrous images" of his awakening consciousness of the body. Masturbation guilt sweeps over him. Yet the shock of the word *"Foetus,"* unloosing the "infuriated cries within him" and closing his ears to his father's wearisome voice, is a salutary one. The nameless and speechless foetus is a challenge to his own knowledge of origin and personal identity; and, in response to the challenge, Stephen speaks his name to himself:

> —I am Stephen Dedalus. I am walking beside my father whose name is Simon Dedalus. We are in Cork, in Ireland. Cork is a city. Our room is in the Victoria Hotel. Victoria and Stephen and Simon. Simon and Stephen and Victoria. Names.

His memory of his childhood grows dim; all he can recall are the names. But then, cut off from the child that he once was, he begins to tell himself the story of that "little boy in a grey belted suit." For the space of a paragraph he becomes a deliberate autobiographer, recalling the geography lessons he had from Dante, his experiences at Clongowes and his impressions and sensations in the infirmary. Notably absent from this mini-autobiography is any mention of his immediate family. The omission makes his story that of one who, as Simon's friend Johnny Cashman hints, is "not his father's son"—a small ex-boarding school boy who was once a nameless foetus. In this mood he has, however, two new resources. One is a "cold and cruel and loveless lust." The other is literature. Stephen is able to salve his bitterness and despair by repeating some lines of Shelley. And so this disturbing episode ends by confirming his ability to oppose the written word (his own and others') to the hollowsounding voices around him.

Stephen, however, still has to cope with the explosion of consciousness represented by the word *"Foetus."* In giving way to his sexual desires he is unloosing the "cry that he had strangled for so long in his throat." Degrading though it may be, his visit to the whore restores the human contact that he has missed ever since his knowledge of his father's failure began to impinge on his innocent days with Uncle Charles. Stephen is tongue-tied once again in the young woman's room, but it is her physical gestures more than her words—touching his arm, ruffling his hair, and undoing her gown—which bring him into a state of peace with his body. For the first time since childhood he becomes aware of speech, not as disembodied admonition but as a vehicle of empathy with another person. With her kiss, he seems to pass beyond the world of "hollowsounding voices" to the root of speech:

> He closed his eyes, surrendering himself to her, body and
> mind, conscious of nothing in the world but the dark
> pressures of her softly parting lips. They pressed upon his
> brain as upon his lips as though they were the vehicle of a
> vague speech; and between them he felt an unknown and
> timid pressure, darker than the swoon of sin, softer than
> sound or odour.

Stephen has been segregated from female influence during his
adolescence; now the physical reality of the woman bursts on him
like a revelation. Such a blissful escape from the realms of socially
acceptable voice and speech cannot possibly be allowed to last. He
feels he has transgressed the social order and that the "squalor and
insincerity" he had felt around him have taken possession of his own
mind. In a heightened version of the movement we have observed in
Dubliners, the rapture of the kiss is succeeded by the sense of sin and
the agonies of penitence. In the next chapter the whore's penetration
of Stephen's brain and soul is cauterized by Father Arnall's pungent
sermons. Father Arnall's is a paternal voice far more compelling in its
sway over the adolescent mind than that of Stephen's natural father.
Through his eloquence the text itself is pervaded by the crushing
authority of the Church.

Catholic and Protestant readers alike have responded to this
chapter in which Joyce—like such near-contemporaries as Dosto-
yevsky and D. H. Lawrence—exposes traditional Christianity not as
a religion of love but one based on torture, fear and self-mortification.
Stephen's combination of imaginative power and newly awakened
sensuality makes him an easy prey for the preacher's morbid evocation
of physical disgust. His early sexual experience was an attempt to
appease a sort of soul-hunger, a longing to escape from the banalities
of existence represented by his father and his schoolmates; but the
Church is far better qualified than the red-light district to offer a
genuine "other world" beyond theirs. Stephen's first sexual rapture
has long faded when the retreat begins, and—echoing Shelley's fragment which he voiced in the previous chapter—he is again subject to
"weariness" and the solitude of an empty, chaotic universe. Catholicism repopulates the universe with heaven and hell, reward and
punishment, presided over by the Virgin "whose emblem is the
morning star." For Stephen, this revelation of the imaginative depths

of the religion he has been brought up in since childhood is irresistible. There is nothing surprising about his agonies of penitence.

Father Arnall's sermons are the product of the literary tradition of "spiritual exercises" deriving from St Ignatius Loyola, the founder of the Jesuit order. Their authority over Stephen, however, owes everything to oral delivery and can best be described in the phrase Joyce used for the artist's endeavour in his essay "A Portrait of the Artist": these are sermons which conclusively "give the word." Yet in writing them into his novel Joyce was embarking on a Swiftian or Voltairean philosophical exercise, designed to expose the contradictions and absurdity of the traditional view of the terrors of hell. In the measure that Stephen becomes enthralled by the voice of the priest, so should the reader become immune to it. Starting out from the commonplaces of Christian doctrine, the sermons tease out the implications of these doctrines with a literalness and realism which amount in the end to a grotesque perversion of reason. When Father Arnall discourses on eternity, for example, his purpose is to make the brain "reel dizzily," in fact to torture it. The more vivid the listener's imagination, the more he is likely to be stunned and—given the social authority vested in the Church—inoculated against any further questioning of the eternal verities. Would not such a questioner, a potential heretic, be like the little bird coming to the mountain, "reaching from the earth to the farthest heavens" for its grain of sand in the knowledge that the mountain will rise again and again even after his puny intellect has succeeded in demolishing it? Yet, from another point of view, the technique of the sermons is surprisingly crude and indiscriminate: for all their eloquence and ingenuity, in their resort to terrorizing the audience and in their deliberate confusion of literal and metaphorical statements they come close to absurdity. So far as terror and intimidation are concerned, they invite the response of the English master, in a brief respite between sermons:

> —I suppose he rubbed it into you well.
> —You bet he did. He put us all into a blue funk.
> —That's what you fellows want: and plenty of it to make you work.

The master's healthy cynicism suggests that religion is no more than social cement, an "opium of the people." The priest's voice encourages the boys to get on with their work by discouraging idle speculation; it is an aversion therapy designed to make thinking for oneself seem painful and profitless. Stephen's reaction is an extreme example of such a conditioned reflex. Father Arnall says that, bad as are the physical punishments of the damned, their worst torments are mental and result from unappeasable remorse and from envy of the blessed from whose good fortune they are eternally excluded. Memory and imagination, the very faculties which distinguish Stephen from his fellows, thus become the most refined instruments of infernal torture.

Stephen confesses his sins, though not—significantly—to one of the priests at Belvedere College. Joyce uses the imagery of physical evacuation ("The last sins oozed forth, sluggish, filthy"), but the sins sound paltry once they are put in words, and the "old and weary voice" of the Capuchin priest betrays that he is too worldly-wise to expect that the penitent will give up his sins—they will recur as inevitably as the body secretes fluids. This priest represents another face of the church, not the inhuman rigour of "spiritual exercises" but the promise of communion and spiritual peace in exchange for penitence and submission to authority.

As he went through the back streets of Dublin in search of the chapel where he could make his anonymous confession, Stephen felt a brief reverence for the poor people around him. His communion, however, is taken within the privileged circle of Belvedere College. He goes to Mass with the comfortable thought that a substantial breakfast awaits him at home. Earlier in the chapter this would have been a sign of gluttony, one of the deadly sins into which he has fallen; now it is taken as a sign of grace:

> White pudding and eggs and sausages and cups of tea.
> How simple and beautiful was life after all!

So Joyce's irony undercuts Stephen's penitence. Purged of the cries of self-assertion that arose within him, he has rejoined the Church, and at the same time reestablished his right to enjoy his bourgeois comforts. He says Amen to the words of the service and—in an ending which parallels the kiss of the previous chapter—raises the host to his lips.

The fourth chapter begins with Stephen's display of religious piety which, far from appeasing his soul-hunger, leads to a "sensation of spiritual dryness." Since Joyce will end this chapter with an epiphany on Dollymount Beach, it is notable that he begins by showing Stephen metaphorically stranded and beached. The "flood of temptation" remains well away from his dry shore; but at the end of the chapter he will master his aquaphobia and walk out towards the passionate tides across the sands of Dublin Bay. He does so in obedience to a voice which is neither that of his father nor the Church—a voice which we do not, perhaps, need the authority of a quotation from Newman to identify as the *"voice of Nature."*

Nature, his sense of what is innate to him, is Stephen's chief reason for refusing to train for the priesthood. The words of the subtle and urbane director of Belvedere are unable to inspire him with a sense of vocation, a sense that he has been "called." We see both the inevitability of Stephen's refusal and his own limited understanding of the step he has taken. His decision to try for university pleases his father but confirms an unspoken breach with his mother. What he does not know is that he is about to receive another "call," and that his path will be determined by a spiritual experience as overwhelming as any call to the priesthood. The final section of the chapter is a sustained poetic rhapsody in which every prompting of the external world and of his own nature points towards his becoming an artist.

It is on Dollymount Beach that, as he would later put it, Stephen's "soul is born." Whatever its earlier stirrings, only now can he say that "His soul had arisen from the grave of boyhood, spurning her graveclothes." (The image is again reminiscent of Ibsen's *When We Dead Awaken.*) Joyce affirms the birth of the soul in a rich, vibrant and sonorous prose which marks the culmination of the romantic vision of artisthood expressed in the *Portrait*. The section contains many mingled strains of poetic imagery: evocations of the sands and the sea, of clouds and flight, and of noises and names are interwoven to create a rapturous and spellbinding symphony in words. The verbal symphony attempts to give sound and substance to the single inarticulate "cry" which Stephen himself experiences— a cry which comes forth both from deep within himself and from the natural world around him:

> His throat ached with a desire to cry aloud, the cry of a hawk or eagle on high, to cry piercingly of his deliverance to the winds. This was the call of life to his soul not the dull gross voice of the world of duties and despair, nor the inhuman voice that had called him to the pale service of the altar. An

instant of wild flight had delivered him and the cry of triumph which his lips withheld cleft his brain.

The references to voices in this extract are developed throughout the beach episode. The voice of the world of duties is represented by his father's "shrill whistle" which he expects to call him back, by the tramping of the squad of Christian Brothers whose names Stephen hears (or imagines hearing) on the bridge, and by the banter of his bathing schoolfellows. Set against these outer voices is the inner music which resounds in Stephen himself: an "elfin prelude," a "chord," "a confused music within him as of memories and names which he was almost conscious of but could not capture even for an instant." The music, however, issues in words: "He felt his cheeks aflame and his throat throbbing with song." Two symbols, the birdlike girl and the hawklike man, express the communion between Stephen's own nature and the wild nature around him. He is "crying to greet the advent of the life that had cried to him," and his cry is summed up in words which suggest a transferred religious ecstasy, a "nature-worship" such as is found in the novels of Meredith and D. H. Lawrence:

—Heavenly God! cried Stephen's soul, in an outburst of profane joy.

Stephen has rejected the priesthood but has by no means dispensed with broadly religious categories of experience.

The beach episode illustrates Matthew Arnold's influential contrast of Hebraism and Hellenism—of Christian revelation and artistic "sweetness and light"—and it is no accident that the voice of nature speaks partly through Greek symbols and emblems. Stephen's fellow-students unwittingly introduce the Hellenistic motif when they offer back his name in a Greek form: "—Stephanos Dedalos! Bous Stephanoumenos! Bous Stephaneforos!" Daedalus, the inventor of flight, manifests the artist's ability to create "a new soaring impalpable imperishable being," akin to the "dappled seaborne clouds" which can travel in reality where Stephen can only go in his imagination. The girl in midstream, who seems "like one whom magic had changed into the likeness of a strange and beautiful seabird," is both a secular angel and a manifestation of the Muse as she would appear to the Daedalian or wingéd artist. The chastity of Stephen's vision as he contemplates the girl in this annunciation-

scene is both wholly convincing and in sharp contrast to other
visions of beach-girls and girls with their skirts pinned up in Joyce:
not only Gerty MacDowell, the modern Nausicaa whose self-display
is watched by the tired businessman Leopold Bloom in *Ulysses,* but
also the women conjured up earlier in this chapter by the rector's
joke about bicycling priests.

Stephen at the end of the fourth chapter has, as it were, taken his
vows and become an artist. Artisthood for him appears as a vocation
or state, not as a process of achievement, so that he can glory in
possessing it long before he has produced any artistic works. To
artisthood as a vocation he transfers the dedication and religious
ardour that conventionally pertain to the priesthood. He has ex-
changed the spiritual dryness of his days as a neophyte Christian for
the spiritual (and possibly physical) state of "dewy wetness" in
which he later prepares to compose his villanelle.

Stephen now tends to cast the Church as his enemy and rival.
Particularly telling is his jealousy of Father Moran, the priest with
whom he suspects his "beloved" of flirting in the Irish language class
in the fifth chapter. The priest, Stephen contemptuously tells himself,
is "but schooled in the discharging of a formal rite," whereas he, the
artist, is a "priest of eternal imagination, transmuting the daily bread
of experience into the radiant body of everliving life." This is a very
transparent conception, which reveals a veneration of eternity reminiscent of Father Arnall and his sermon. The stage of self-liberation
that Stephen has reached at the end of the *Portrait* (and the same may
be said of Joyce at the age when he began to write) is that of staking
everything on his sense of belonging to a heretical priesthood, the
custodians of the "religion of art." At the same time he has begun the
process of intellectual and emotional hardening destined to make him
very different from the languorous fin-de-siècle poets who were his
predecessors in turning art into an object of worship. The "Villanelle
of the Temptress" that is Stephen's principal literary composition in
the fifth chapter marks his homage to the Decadent school. Many of
the Decadent poets, as is well known, recanted their aesthetic
heresies and ended their days back in the bosom of the Church. By
the end of the *Portrait* we are beginning—but no more than beginning—to perceive that Stephen may be made of sterner stuff.

The third and fourth chapters have taken place largely in the
theatre of Stephen's consciousness—a theatre, however, which
echoes with a few commanding voices from outside, and notably the

voice of Father Arnall. The presentation of Stephen's university life restores the sense of human variety and the breadth of social perspective which were absent from these chapters. For a time, Stephen listens acutely to the voices around him, though by the end he has withdrawn into diary-keeping, and listening has given place to writing. It is hard to do justice to the variety and rich modulations of this chapter, which introduces a number of characters with the greatest economy of gesture and contains some of Joyce's liveliest and most memorable dialogues. Much as he may despise his fellow-students Stephen tends to make them into larger-than-life figures, representatives of the major attitudes at work in the society around him. Of Davin, for example, Stephen reflects that "the gossip of his fellowstudents which strove to render the flat life of the college significant at any cost loved to think of him as a young fenian." Stephen is as adept as any of his fellows at giving a legendary quality to the flat life of the college, at least to the extent that it impinges on him. It is true that this portrait is an unflattering one, which did not please everybody. Maud Gonne, the Irish revolutionary, wrote in 1917 that "those who know the young students in Dublin, the intensity and vividness of their lives . . . would find it hard to recognise the uncouth nonentities presented by Joyce." Posterity, it must be confessed, tends to prefer Joyce's "uncouth nonentities" to Maud Gonne's brand of high-minded zealots.

Stephen begins the chapter by driving the voices of his father, his mother, and the mad nun out of his heart with an execration. For the time being these are supplanted by a new set of voices: those of his friends, and also the silent voices ("silence" is a key word in this chapter) of the literary tradition. Walking to college, he thinks in turn of the words of Gerhart Hauptmann, Newman, Cavalcanti, Ibsen and one of Ben Jonson's songs—in itself a remarkable display of intellectual precocity on Stephen's part. Beyond this there is the philosophical task he has given himself, that of deriving a theory of beauty from some sentences of Aristotle and Aquinas, even though their learning is "held no higher by the age he lived in than the subtle and curious jargons of heraldry and falconry."

If literature and philosophy are portals of discovery they can also serve as defence mechanisms, helping to shut out the noise of his environment. The same is true of his conspicuous adoption of the role of the poet: it forces him to justify himself, and at the same time protects him against the claims of the more assertive of his fellow-students. It is both amusing and, in the light of Ireland's subsequent history, deeply instructive to see how Stephen evades the challenges represented by three of these, MacCann, Davin and MacAlister, by playing off each against the others. MacCann is collecting signatures for a universal disarmament petition, *"Pax super totum sanguinarium globum"* as Cranly mockingly puts it. Stephen's refusal to sign is characteristic and yet not easy to justify (Joyce, after all, never wavered in his detestation of militarism and violence). He discredits the petition by remarking that Davin, the "fenian," has signed; Davin in his simplicity can find no contradiction between universal peace and armed rebellion in the cause of Ireland. Davin is the most likeable of the student ideologists, but Stephen exposes him (and with him a whole strain of Irish nationalism) as incorrigibly sentimental and given to self-deception. Davin's well-meant confusion reflects ironically on the idealism of MacCann, who believes that the petition is a step on the road to a new millennium of universal altruism. MacAlister, the Ulster Catholic, is the least sympathetic of the three characters under consideration. His attitude to knowledge is crassly utilitarian, he accuses Stephen of intellectual crankery, and (worst of all) he has a grating Belfast accent. Stephen is irritated by him to the point of "bidding his mind think that the student's father would have done better had he sent his son to Belfast to study and have saved something on the train fare by so doing." Another student, Moynihan, calls MacAlister "a devil for his pound of flesh"; and it is perhaps the self-righteousness implicit in this remark which persuades Stephen to swallow his own irritation: "Can you say with certitude by whom the soul of your race was bartered and its elect betrayed—by the questioner or by the mocker?" he reflects.

Treachery, in Stephen's view, is an inescapable part of Ireland's heritage. The belief that the Irish invariably betray one another is one of his justifications for washing his hands of his native country. Later, the same belief sustained Joyce's own habitual cynicism about Irish politics. Parnell's fate, on this view, was both predictable in itself and a warning to all his potential successors. Moreover, the betrayers are not necessarily the utilitarian northerners, the West Britons or those most infected by English values. Sentimental, self-righteous southern Republicans also have a history of treachery. Whatever we think of Stephen's (and Joyce's) political disenchantment, he cannot be accused of being pro-English. H. G. Wells, reading the *Portrait* at much the same time as Maud Gonne (that is, within a year of the 1916 Easter Rising) noted that "everyone in this story, every human being, accepts as a matter of course, as a thing in nature like the sky and the sea, that the English are to be hated." But Stephen's attitudes grow out of his experiences in childhood and youth which have taught him that the ideological voices of his fellow-students, like the earlier voices of duty and moral exhortation, are so many snares and nets. He says to Davin, "You talk to me of nationality, language, religion. I shall try to fly by those nets."

Stephen's search for spiritual freedom coexists with an extreme defensive anxiety to secure himself against the possibility of betrayal. This is the rationale behind his watchwords "silence exile and cunning" and also, I suspect, behind his theory of aesthetic "stasis" in which the mind is "arrested and raised above desire and loathing." The static work of art is by definition silent—eloquently silent, no doubt, like Keats's Grecian Urn—but still the opposite of a voice exhorting its hearer to take some action. Stephen's dedication to silence is not yet complete, since he still feels able to confess his feelings to friends such as Davin and Cranly. It is Cranly who first hears of his refusal to make his Easter duty, which opens a breach between him and his mother and is his first unequivocal act of rebellion. Cranly is a shrewd listener, telling Stephen how curiously his mind is "supersaturated with the religion in which you say you disbelieve." Beneath his hardboiled exterior he shows considerable affection for Stephen, and is vividly aware of the loneliness to which his rebellion will bring him. Yet Stephen also constructs an imaginary romance between Cranly and Emma, the shadowy girl from his adolescence to whom he still feels emotionally drawn. It is as if he has singled out Cranly from the other students only to force him into the mould of the betrayer.

Is he, then, perfecting himself as an artist at the (necessary) expense of the human relationships Dublin could offer? If so, the exhilarating cry of "Welcome, O life!" with which the *Portrait* ends must be read as a triumphant announcement that Stephen has fulfilled his artistic novitiate. This would imply that artisthood is indeed the noblest of vocations and that—as with the priesthood—the world is well lost for it. There is, however, another less exalted and religiose view of the artist which serves as an implicit corrective to Stephen's effusions, and as a source of irony. (The irony, of course, is very much more patent when we think of Stephen as he appears in *Ulysses*.) A priest is judged by what he is—by the state of his soul—but an artist must earn his title by what he creates or produces. Stephen takes it for granted that he commands the privileges of the artist, though his title to them rests on a distinctly meagre performance in the present, and an unknown promise for the future.

In accordance with this ironic perspective, Stephen's actual development as a writer in the *Portrait* is a mixture of real discoveries and false starts. In part we see him as an *epiphanist*, recording the manifestations of beauty he encounters. He collects a "garner of slender sentences" from Aristotle and Aquinas and some less exalted phrases from the Elizabethan lutanists. Instructed by his dabblings in theosophy he looks out for natural symbols, such as the returning swallows he sees and hears outside the National Library—creatures which are "in the order of their life and have not perverted that order by reason." These are Yeatsian sentiments, and in turn they evoke the death-speech from Yeats's play *The Countess Cathleen,* which Stephen has witnessed at the disastrous opening of the national theatre:

> *Bend down your faces, Oona and Aleel,*
> *I gaze upon them as the swallow gazes*
> *Upon the nest under the eave before*
> *He wander the loud waters.*

> A soft liquid joy like the noise of many waters flowed over his memory and he felt in his heart the soft peace of silent spaces of fading tenuous sky above the waters, of oceanic silence, of swallows flying through the seadusk over the flowing waters.

Like several other passages towards the end of the *Portrait,* this has the deliberate air of an epiphany. The "soft liquid joy"—wetness— is reminiscent of the much more extended sequence in which he is inspired to compose the villanelle. At the same time the imagery is almost identical with that of Poem 35 of *Chamber Music:*

> All day I hear the noise of waters
>   Making moan
> Sad as the seabird is when going
>   Forth alone
> He hears the winds cry to the waters'
>   Monotone.

> The grey winds, the cold winds are blowing
> > Where I go.
> I hear the noise of many waters
> > Far below.
> All day, all night, I hear them flowing
> > To and fro.

This fine lyric, severely modelled on a verse-form of Verlaine's, is a much more genuine achievement than the self-conscious "symbol of departure or of loneliness" in the *Portrait*. In it the poet *is* the seabird. In the prose passage, however, the lush word-painting comes close to absurdity. "Oceanic silence" is an oxymoron, and the "soft liquid joy" seems to be produced, in the end, by no more than Stephen's intoxicated contemplation of his own words: "A soft liquid joy flowed through the words where the soft long vowels hurtled noiselessly and fell away, lapping and flowing back and ever shaking the white bells of their waves in mute chime and mute peal and soft low swooning cry." But this is only one of the directions in which Stephen's precocious intelligence is turning.

Stephen's aesthetic theory both extends and distorts what has earlier been put forward in *Stephen Hero*. Once again Joyce sets it out with a curious blend of autobiography and fictional artifice. Speaking to Lynch, Stephen claims to be quoting from a "book at home" in which he has written down a series of questions. These questions may be found in the "Paris notebook" in which Joyce made signed and dated entries in 1903—a year *after* his graduation from University College. In the *Portrait*, Stephen opposes "kinetic" to "static" art, redefines *integritas, consonantia* and *claritas,* and then distinguishes between the lyrical, epical and dramatic forms of art. Stephen's definition of *claritas* or radiance—the key to his theory of beauty— has a quite different emphasis to the one he offered in *Stephen Hero*. He starts by disavowing symbolism or idealism, in the ninetyish or Yeatsian sense of "the supreme quality of beauty being a light from some other world." That would, perhaps, be a too obviously mystical or religious view of art for Stephen to espouse. In its place, he offers a lyrical account of the experience of artistic inspiration. The supreme quality of beauty "is felt by the artist when the esthetic image is first conceived in his imagination." Shelley's comparison of the mind in creation to a fading coal, and the physiologist Galvani's description of a cardiac condition "called the enchantment of the heart," are thrown in by way of elaboration. All this is profoundly evasive, a mystification of the artistic process which gives no indication of the sources of the all-important "esthetic image." Shelley, as a neoplatonist, *would* have believed that the image is a light from some other world. Aquinas likewise would argue that our ability to respond to earthly beauty is divinely inspired. Stephen can merely speak of an "enchantment of the heart" without saying by whom or what the poet is made open to enchantment. The answer is implicit in the following episode—in which he composes the "Villanelle of the Temptress"—but Stephen does not manage to formulate it theoretically. In the villanelle episode the poet is enchanted by the "Temptress" or muse, and she in turn is a figment of his own brain. Because his brain is still supersaturated with the Catholic religion, the "Temptress" is also the Virgin Mary. For the same reason, Stephen in the *Portrait* is unable to evolve a satisfactory theory of artistic creation. One indication of its unsatisfactoriness is that he unceremoniously abandons it, in favour of a wholly different and much more materialistic approach, which he expounds (using Shakespeare as his text) in the Library chapter of *Ulysses*.

Stephen has more success in the *Portrait* as a theorist of literary genres. Indeed, his distinction between the lyrical, epical, and dramatic forms has possibly attracted as much comment as the rest of the book put together. My interest at present is simply to read it as a commentary on Stephen's (and Joyce's) artistic development, which is clearly a progression from the lyrical to the dramatic. The lyrical form is "the simplest verbal vesture of an instant of emotion, a rhythmical cry such as ages ago cheered on the man who pulled at the oar or dragged stones up a slope. He who utters it is more conscious of the instant of emotion than of himself as feeling emotion." Stephen has uttered many such cries in the course of his childhood and adolescence, and with the composition of the villanelle he shows himself capable of a highly sophisticated, verbally elaborate rhythmical cry. But also, "the simplest epical form is seen emerging out of lyrical literature when the artist prolongs and broods upon himself as the centre of an epical event and this form progresses till the centre of gravity is equidistant from the artist himself and from others." Stephen from childhood has been shown constituting himself as an autobiographer, brooding upon his own development as the centre of an epical event. The process involves detachment of the "personality of the artist," which "passes into the narration itself" and thus becomes separable from the character of the hero, though not always unambiguously so. Stephen's emergence as an autobiographical artist remains quite incomplete, since it can only be fulfilled by the writing of the *Portrait* itself. The third stage—the dramatic form which is realized when "the vitality which has flowed and eddied round each person fills every person with such vital force that he or she assumes a proper and intangible esthetic life"—is still more a prophecy for the future.

Read in this way, Stephen's theory of literary genres serves to rationalize Joyce's development, rendering a unique and perhaps fortuitous process as classical and inevitable. The symbols and prophecies which herald Stephen's emergence as an artist have the same effect. The *Portrait* as a whole is the outcome of a long romantic tradition of special pleading on behalf of the artist. Joyce's absorbing and utterly convincing picture of Stephen's childhood and youth persuades us of the inevitability and poetic justice of his later specialization. At the same time, the *Portrait* cuts itself off from the ideal of the fully rounded human personality. Karl Marx imagined a non-alienated society in which the fulfilled man would be able to hunt in the morning, fish in the afternoon, rear cattle in the evening and be a critical critic after dinner. Such a life would be meaningless to Stephen, whose whole identity is founded on the idea of a predestined, priestlike vocation. It would, however, suit Leopold Bloom who already lives a bourgeois version of the all-round life. The *Portrait,* though one of the most brilliant of early twentieth-century novels, would seem distinctly one-sided did it not also serve as a prologue to *Ulysses*.

In the *Portrait* two views of the artist—the Dedalian view that he is born and the more conventional view that he must prove himself by what he makes—are held in a subtle dialectic. The latter view, though unstated, is the basis of the narrator's ironic detachment. There is, however, an implied resolution of the dialectic in the notion that Stephen is the future author of an achieved work of art, the *Portrait of the Artist,* which largely vindicates the high claims he has made. Or can it be that the formative experiences that would show him how to *write about* his childhood belong in the future, and are as yet unforeseen? The ending of the *Portrait* is delicately balanced between these two interpretations. The final pages are in the form of a writer's notebook. The first entry is dated March 20 and is a memorandum of a talk with Cranly, the dramatized version of which we have already read. Here the bridge between Stephen as protagonist and Stephen as autobiographer is deliberately crossed. The three concluding notebook entries form a coda terminating the novel in exquisitely musical fashion, in which the dialectic of "voices" and "cries" is brought to a triumphant resolution. The restraining voice of his mother, reminding him "what the heart is and what it feels," is set against the "spell of arms and voices"—those of imaginary kinsmen, like the temptress he has conjured up in his villanelle; siren voices beckoning him away from home with their "tale of distant nations." Stephen resolves the conflict with a final invocation of his "Old father, old artificer"—primarily his adopted mentor Daedalus, but carrying an inevitable implied salute to the real father, whose stature has fallen steadily during the course of the narrative only to rise again, as the storyteller with whose voice it all began. "In my end is my beginning"—for, to begin his task as autobiographer, Stephen will have to write an opening paragraph in which he adopts his father's voice.

Such an interpretation is momentarily satisfying, presenting the *Portrait* as a closed and circular narrative in the manner of *Finnegans Wake*. But it overlooks both the imminence of *Ulysses,* which in some respects is a genuine sequel to the *Portrait,* and also the actual texture of the last few pages of notebook entries. Most of these are disparate, inconsequential, and inharmonious. Stephen's tone is frequently brittle, posturing, and unstable. Far from knowing what he is looking for, he is setting down "epiphanies" of a very varied kind which just might be worked up into something substantial. Is this the artist who is ready to "forge in the smithy of my soul the uncreated conscience of my race"? The answer must be that he is still at the stage of life when his ambition outruns his capabilities. With Emma, for example, he makes "a sudden gesture of a revolutionary nature. I must have looked like a fellow throwing a handful of peas into the air." The gesture is premature and out of place—but at least Stephen himself can see the irony of it. Emma, it is clear, regards him as something of an exhibitionist rather than revering him as an artist. His chapter-ending cry of "Welcome, O life!"—repeated, as we have seen, for the fifth time—does not of itself guarantee that Stephen will achieve the deliverance he seeks. In this sense the *Portrait* is open-ended. The young artist's rejection of family and friends will lead him not to assured international fame but to the Martello Tower and the voices he will hear in *Ulysses.*

Monte Cristo's Revenge and Joyce's *A Portrait of the Artist*

Michael Seidel

"Out of the Land of Egypt into the House of Bondage"

Stephen Dedalus has his moments of exultation in *A Portrait of the Artist,* but he is at his most controlled and calculated when he inaugurates his long-range defensive program for aesthetic revenge: "silence, exile, and cunning." His program bears an inverse relation to the qualities exhibited by Irish stay-at-homes—palaver, paralysis, and sentimentality—in the first book that James Joyce completed in *his* European exile, *Dubliners.*

Exile is the least odd of the three strategies; even if its end remains unclear, it can, at least, be located as a tactic. Joyce became an exile; he titled his one play *Exiles;* and he absorbed the most renowned of exilic themes, the Odyssean wanderings, into the texture of both his Irish epics. In the comic spectacle of *Finnegans Wake,* the artist Shem is a perpetual inscriber and a perpetual resettler (a "sooner") whose subject is his own sustenance in exile: "He even ran away with hunself and became a farsoonerite, saying he would far sooner muddle through the hash of lentils in Europe than meddle with Irrland's split little pea." Shem the Penman makes exile into a form of autobiography, "self exiled in upon his ego."

Silence and cunning, as befit them, are less easily revealed as Joycean impulses. It is difficult to guess exactly what Stephen means

From *Exile and the Narrative Imagination.* © 1986 by Yale University. Yale University Press, 1986.

by them unless we align the terms with attributes of narrative design—surely the Odyssean one and, more pointedly, the Daedalian one. Like Odysseus on Calypso's island at the western extreme of the Mediterranean, Daedalus near its eastern extreme on Minos's Crete already suffers exile as part of his fate; he need not enjoin its necessity. Silence and cunning, therefore, are means to effect an exilic alternative, a Greek *nostos*. For the young Stephen Dedalus, of course, England's King Edward takes a less active interest in his affairs than the Cretan King Minos takes in those of Daedalus; nor is the Irish Catholic church so alluring a bride as Odysseus's island-binding goddess Calypso. Joyce's Dedalus must effect his problem before he can render its solution.

If in *Portrait* Joyce talks up the aesthetic program before the exilic adventure, in his play, *Exiles,* Joyce advances the cisatlantic connection beyond the point of exilic return. "Why the title *Exiles?*" he asks in a note to his play, and he answers his own question: "A nation exacts a penance from those who dared to leave her payable on their return." Joyce goes on to note that only in the otherworldly wisdom of the biblical prodigal son story is the voluntary exile honored at home—"certainly not in Ireland." In *Ulysses,* Stephen Dedalus hints in the telegram he sends Buck Mulligan—a phrase cribbed from Meredith's *Ordeal of Richard Feverel:* "—*The sentimentalist is he who would enjoy without incurring the immense debtorship for a thing done*"—that the only debt worth repaying is the one worth incurring. But it is crucial to recognize that for Joyce the notion of Irish debt has little to do with the dare of nationalist politics or the glory of Ireland's national cultural revival, at least in the usual way these issues were conceived, and much more to do with the redemptive exilic structures that underwrite the particular Joycean narrative enterprise. In *Exiles,* the returned writer, Richard, marks as worthless Robert's article in honor of his repatriation in Ireland because it contains a phrase about "those who left her in her hour of need." All Ireland's hours are her hours of need, and loyalty to lost causes is decidedly not the penance that Joyce would pay, though such might have been the penance the native Irish would most want to exact from him. Dedalus made this point in *Portrait:* "—My ancestors threw off their language and took another, Stephen said. They allowed a handful of foreigners to subject them. Do you fancy I am going to pay in my own life and person debts they made? What for?"

In distinction to Richard Rowan's exile in the play, Joyce's own exile "dared" remain permanent. But did Joyce feel he still owed anything? And, if so, to whom? The penance Joyce reveals himself most willing to pay Ireland is the only return on his overseas investment that he deems worth anything, a return that contributes to Ireland a stock of literary increase as abundant as the booty Odysseus brought back to redeem a destitute Ithaca. He calls this in *Finnegans Wake* the burden carried by "our homerole poet to Ostelinda," where home rule becomes a Homeric project and the Mediterranean adventure merges into a Norse saga. In *Stephen Hero,* Joyce's still diphthonged young Daedalus comments on the enlightened impulse of modern secular art that distances itself from presumptive States, Redeemers, and Churches: "It examines the entire community in action and reconstructs the spectacle of redemption." Redemption is a making good after going out on account, and if Joyce, as Ireland's unreturned prodigal, ends up practicing any of what his first Daedalus preached, he pays up, in a fashion, by the full communal spectacle he represents in and with his exilic narratives.

One of the more expansive glosses on exilic redemption occurs in "Aeolus" in *Ulysses* (the only passage for which we have an extant recorded reading by Joyce) when Professor MacHugh recalls John F. Taylor's speech in response to Mr. Justice Fitzgibbon on the question of reviving the Irish tongue. Clearly, this was an issue that rallied nationalist fervor and constituted in most palpable terms the redemptive impulse of a culture that deemed itself in exilic bondage while another nation controlled its fate. "We were weak, therefore worthless" says Professor MacHugh about to recite Taylor's oratorical comparison of the Irish to the Israelites. Had Moses bowed before Egypt,

> he would never have brought the chosen people out of their house
> of bondage, nor followed the pillar of the cloud by day. He would
> never have spoken with the Eternal amid lightnings on Sinai's
> mountaintop nor ever have come down with the light of inspira-
> tion shining in his countenance and bearing in his arms the tables
> of the law, graven in the language of the outlaw.

When in *Portrait of the Artist,* Cranly was trying to persuade Dedalus to consider the range of options open to him at home, he argued that he need not look upon himself as "an outlaw" in Ireland. But by *Ulysses* that was precisely what appeared essential in terms of the exilic pattern Joyce extracted from the narrative histories with which he worked, the "epic of two races (Israelite—Irish)," and the *Ulysses* myth transposed, as Joyce put it, *"sub specie temporis nostri."* Though Joyce had little sympathy for the issue that forms the Israelite homology for Taylor and MacHugh, the revival of the Gaelic tongue, he found absorbing the notion that the meaning of a land's destiny could derive from the range and full force of inscription, conceived in language that opened the national adventure for a variety of narrative adaptations: allusive, parodic, prophetic, homiletic, and, by the time of *Finnegans Wake,* syllabic.

Stephen Dedalus's first public voicing in *Ulysses,* his "Pisgah Sight of Palestine," based on what has gone on so far during his day, comes as a rival vision to Taylor's oratory: "—I have a vision too." Later, when the professor suggests the Latin title *"Deus nobis haec otia fecit,"* Stephen insists on the Old Testament parody of a different prospect, the view from the exilic spaces of the promised land. The elongated Latin pun "periplum" (or island circuit) in Stephen's subtitle "Parable of the Plums," perhaps gets some of the classical element back, enabling Stephen to confront all Mediterranean precursors, to satisfy or fulfill the range of the material available to him. His effort, feebly funny, represents, as many have pointed out, the first time that he has positioned himself for an enterprise that incorporates most of the elements that contribute to Joyce's larger and later narrative efforts: the detailed stuff of his home city; the lore of exilic imagining; the parody of urban nostos. Naturally enough, the first word of Stephen's international parable is "Dubliners." The duplication of the home space as the wandering space assumed by the parable indicates the enlarged and enlarging role of exilic parody for Joyce when the "rock" of narration no longer affords complete haven for the rooted consciousness of voice and when, as Stephen's parable implies, Dublin itself becomes at once alien and visionary ground.

There is, of course, another Dubliner in *Ulysses* whose story hovers around the homologic spaces of Palestine, Mr. Leopold Bloom of Eccles Street. Bloom is the son of a man who, in typical formulaic fashion, initiates an actual exilic experience, "who left the house of his father and left the God of his father," whereas Bloom himself must perform a double, or narratively allegoric, service for

Joyce's exilic-redemptive scheme to work in *Ulysses*. In "Aeolus," a throwaway remark by Bloom contains within it the principle of exilic realignment. Bloom misconstrues the biblical Exodus—just as he misconstrues, with similar duplicity, the home rule sun rising in the northwest of Ireland—when he remembers the Pesach service and "that long business about that brought us out of the land of Egypt and into the house of bondage." The exilic Bloom is generated by the very mythology the narrative establishes for him, "Leopold Bloom of no fixed abode" whose exodus from one land of bondage to another is part of his defense in the phantasmagoria of "Circe," "my client's native place, the land of the Pharaoh." The turning of the cliché makes Bloom's Ireland into the space of exile, a poor delivery in an unpromising, hostile land—or a stiff one if we consider the version of Irish delivery actually provided in "Oxen of the Sun"—until and unless Joyce converts the exilic place of wandering into the home place of rest and return in that promised land of "Ithaca."

Garrett Deasy in "Nestor" already condemned the Jews to eternal wandering over the face of the earth, and even Stephen contributes to the exilic myth in regard to Bloom. His thoughts, no doubt, have been touched by Mulligan's reference to Bloom's lusting Galilean eyes, but Stephen (or the text of "Circe" within Stephen's scope at the moment) cannot help making the comparison between Bloom and a local citizen whom everyone calls Dublin's hump-backed Jew. Stephen sees Bloom at the brothel and thinks, "A time, times and half a time," which amounts to his own review of the three times so far in which he knows that he and Bloom have crossed paths: once in the library, once in "Oxen of the Sun," and now (ongoing) in "Circe." With no break but a blank line, we read the Circean stage direction: *Reuben J. Antichrist, wandering jew.*

After "Circe," Bloom and Stephen begin to talk in "Eumaeus," though largely at cross-purposes. The conversation touches upon those recurrent exilic questions: to whom does Ireland belong? and what sort of currency might earn its repossession? Stephen's is an impertinent version of the artist as exile with his Irish belongings on show (impertinent because as yet unrealized).

> You have every bit as much right to live by your pen in
> pursuit of your philosophy as the peasant has. What? You

both belong to Ireland, the brain and the brawn. Each is equally important.

—You suspect, Stephen retorted with a sort of a half laugh, that I may be important because I belong to the *faubourg Saint Patrice* called Ireland for short.

—I would go a step farther, Mr Bloom insinuated.

—But I suspect, Stephen interrupted, that Ireland must be important because it belongs to me.

—What belongs? queried Mr Bloom, bending, fancying he was perhaps under some misapprehension.

Bloom, the outcast and the homebody, supposes Stephen speaks of the political cisatlantic connection—the exilic wild goose—but Stephen intends the principle of exilic resource, even though his efforts to that point have inscribed very little of the Ireland that belongs to him and returned very little of artistic worth to the nation that provides him exilic inspiration. To see how Joyce works with the cross-Atlantic and pan-European adventure, I would like to turn back to *Portrait of the Artist*. Dedalus works through a romantic exilic resource before Joyce discovers a classical Odyssean one.

"Madam, I Never Eat Muscatel Grapes"

The first resourceful plot, indeed the first plot of any kind after the adventures of baby tuckoo and the moocow, that absorbs the young Stephen Dedalus's attention in *Portrait of the Artist* is not the Odyssean adventure that inspired Joyce at the age of twelve but the famous Dumas tale of the exiled Edmond Dantes who reappeared in Europe as the Count of Monte Cristo. Stephen acknowledges only a small part of the story, its renunciatory bravado. He says little of the tale's generative archetypes of great fortune, forbearance, and power. As a fable of exile and return, the whole of the Monte Cristo legend romances the Odyssean epic in bourgeois Europe and, retrospectively, glosses the theory of Shakespearean revenge proposed by an older Dedalus in the library chapter of *Ulysses*. Dumas's tale charts the havoc wreaked by the returned hero on local betrayers. Edmond Dantes is the ghost from *limbo patrum,* the dark avenger who makes retribution into a work of art, who weaves bits and pieces of retributive justice slowly, silently, elaborately into the fabric of a design until, as with the god-inspired interdiction against further Odyssean violence or with the equanimity of Bloom in bed, the Count abjures the very act of revenge as a final flourish preceding exilic rest.

It is this full story—and even the young Stephen presumably knows it, though he focuses on only one of its renunciatory scenes— that touches on the larger Joycean enterprise, the exilic fable that redeems as it disposes, that enlists, the way Bloom later proposes for Stephen, the "equal and opposite power of abandonment and recuperation" (*Ulysses*). As future compositor and assimilator of fragments concerning all those heroes from the "atlantic and Phenitia Proper" (*Finnegans Wake*), Joyce could well revel in the whole of the Monte Cristo legend. Consider its rudiments: a betrayed, abandoned, and returned mariner; an exile sewn into his own shroud and nearly drowned like a swollen bundle in the sea; a European *incog* someone calls an "Oriental, a Levantine, Maltese, Indian, Chinese; your family name is Monte Cristo; Sinbad the Sailor is your baptismal appellation"; the amasser of a personal fortune from the treasure hoard of an Italian prisoner greater than the one Leopold Bloom imagines inheriting from a Spanish prisoner's donation of "a distant treasure of valuables or specie or bullion lodged with a solvent banking corporation 100 years previously at 5% compound interest of the collective worth of £5,000,000 stg" (*Ulysses*); the owner of an eponymous Mediterranean rock-strewn island like the Ionian Ithaca—"this isle is a mass of rocks, and does not contain an acre of land capable of cultivation"; and a Darkinbad Brightdayler whose complexion migrates across the face of Europe, a complexion "so long kept from the sun, had now that pale colour which produces when the features are encircled with black hair the aristocratic beauty of the man of the North."

When the famous Count enters the Joyce canon through the open portals of *Portrait*, the adolescent Dedalus sees him only as a superior avenger, a Byronic hero, an insubstantial lover, a renouncer of corporeal sustenance so that he might gain spiritual control. He exhibits, in short, the grand but weightless romantic temper described by Daedalus in *Stephen Hero:* "blown to wild adventures, lacking the gravity of solid bodies." Stephen's conjuring of Monte Cristo is among his first imaginative projections beyond local borders. As a lad between terms at Clongowes and Belvedere, he spends his long summer days walking with his granduncle in and

around the villages just south of Dublin and his evenings reading
Dumas's massive romance in translation, musing on Edmond
Dantes, Mercedes, and some freshly picked muscatel grapes.

> His evenings were his own; and he pored over a ragged
> translation of *The Count of Monte Cristo*. The figure of that
> dark avenger stood forth in his mind for whatever he had
> heard or divined in childhood of the strange and terrible. At
> night he built up on the parlour table an image of the
> wonderful island cave out of transfers and paper flowers and
> coloured tissue paper and strips of the silver and golden
> paper in which chocolate is wrapped. When he had broken
> up this scenery, weary of its tinsel, there would come to his
> mind the bright picture of Marseilles, of sunny trellisses and
> of Mercedes. Outside Blackrock, on the road that led to the
> mountains, stood a small whitewashed house in the garden
> of which grew many rosebushes: and in this house, he told
> himself another Mercedes lived. Both on the outward and
> on the homeward journey he measured distance by this
> landmark: and in his imagination he lived through a long
> train of adventures, marvelous as those in the book itself,
> towards the close of which there appeared an image of him-
> self, grown older and sadder, standing in a moonlit garden
> with Mercedes who had so many years before slighted his
> love, and with a sadly proud gesture of refusal, saying:
> —Madam, I never eat muscatel grapes.

The young boy's supplemental recall of the Dumas narrative is
what some, in modern day parlance, call a strong reading, that is, an
intentionally mangled one, though the "strong" reading in this case
produces an intentionally "weak" grasp of the matrix of the original.
Stephen's alternation between the libidinal urges of pubescent desire
and the proud freedom of refusal seems to privilege what his more
mature self deems as aesthetically unacceptable kinetic emotions:
"Desire urges us to possess, to go to something; loathing urges us to
abandon, to go from something. These are kinetic emotions." But
we have seen nothing yet, nor are we yet ready, for Stephen the
aesthetician. His boyhood meanderings on the *Monte Cristo* plot
blithely cross into the kinetic domain of self-mythologizing and self-
aggrandizement. He first reproduces the magical place of abundant
treasure, Monte Cristo's island cave, the most powerful evocation of

which comes Kubla Khan–like in the original as the result of a hashish trip; next he places the young Edmond Dantes on the sun-lined streets of Marseilles near his equally young and immensely alluring Mediterranean beauty, Mercedes; finally, Stephen evokes the older, shrewder, and resourceful Monte Cristo (Dantes) in the garden of the vaguely threatened Countess de Morcerf (Mercedes) in Paris.

After the lure of treasure and power, the clearest attraction of the passage for the young Stephen is indeed libidinal. But such an attraction also involves its clearest distortion. He has arrested Mercedes in her own youth or in his unsubstantial understanding of her—she is the "unsubstantial image which his soul so constantly beheld." Though Stephen ages the Count, he has trouble doing the same for Mercedes, and in a later allusion to this same scene we learn he hasn't moved Mercedes to Paris at all; the refusal scene literally takes place where she first appeared as a girl in the Irish Blackrock version of Marseilles: "He saw again the small white house and the garden of rosebushes on the road that led to the mountains and he remembered the sadly proud gesture of refusal which he was to make there, standing with her in the moonlit garden after years of estrangement and adventure." The muscatel grape scene is incorrectly set back at the place and at the time when Mercedes was most delectable. Hers is a sexual offering that Monte Cristo might accept or reject. Renunciation for a boy of Stephen's age is an appropriate control for romance given the amount he might know but the little he could expect from the pleasures of sexual initiation. Mercedes intrigues the young boy as sexual opportunity both available and rejectable, sex, that is, without grapes.

Before focusing on what the actual nature of Monte Cristo's renunciation might mean for the older Stephen, let me reset the scene in its proper perspective. The place and time have nothing to do with a moonlit garden in Marseilles and less to do with a sexual offering than might appear, though the memory of such opportunity certainly contributes to the force of the encounter. Mercedes at the time is a countess in her late thirties and the only person in Paris who has sensed Monte Cristo's real identity. She fears his presence even though she has little sense of the circumstances surrounding his earlier betrayal or the present circumstances surrounding his mysterious reappearance. It is not her own security she fears for, but rather the well-being of her only child, Albert, now a young man. What she senses in Monte Cristo's bearing is the implied threat of exilic or generational revenge for her own action years before in marrying a mere eighteen months after Dantes's imprisonment, an action to which Monte Cristo had applied the troubled Hamlet's remark, breaking into English to do so, "Frailty, thy name is woman" (*The Count of Monte Cristo;* hereafter *MC*).

Mercedes has just coaxed Albert into maneuvering Monte Cristo toward her garden walk in the direction of the greenhouse: " 'The count will never accept an invitation to dine with us,' " she says as she implores Albert to " 'insist upon his taking something.' " Albert demurs but she repeats, as only a mother can, " 'Oblige me, Albert.' " Monte Cristo refuses the son as a kind of prelude for his refusal of the mother. During the stroll to the greenhouse, Mercedes tempts the count with grapes she picks from the vine. " 'Pray excuse me, madame,' replied Monte Cristo, 'but I never eat Muscatel grapes.' " She then offers a peach: no, again. In calculated frustration, Mercedes says, " 'There is a beautiful Arabian custom which makes eternal friends of those who have together eaten bread and salt beneath the same roof.' 'I know it, madam,' replied the count; 'but we are in France, and not in Arabia. And in France eternal friendships are as rare as the custom of sharing bread and salt.' "

Mercedes understands the nature of Monte Cristo's refusal only too well. She reoffers the grapes as a plea for familial safe conduct: " 'Take some.' " Dante refuses, now as an emphatic exercise of his own license to exact whatever revenge he sees fit: " 'Madam, I never eat Muscatel grapes.' " Monte Cristo then concocts a story, an obviously false one, that points his moral and adorns his own tale. He tells of a young girl long in the past who was to wait for him on the isle of Malta but instead married during his absence. In response to Mercedes's question as to whether he had forgiven the girl, Edmond says he had pardoned her, implying, as Mercedes is quick to note, that there might be others whose fate was not—and would not be—so charitably disposed. With a mother's desperation she walks Monte Cristo back in the direction of young Albert and grasps the Count's hands, enfolding them over her son's: " 'We are friends, are we not?' "

As Mercedes leaves the garden, Albert assumes Monte Cristo and his mother have disagreed, and that assumption, at least for the time being, is accurate. Whatever young Stephen sees or misunderstands about the scene in the context of his own desires, it sets a fictional moment in which human bonds are broken, communal ones suspended, and the avenging will given the space to enact its retribution. The refusal to eat, to satisfy or partake under a hostess's roof, allows for the putative romantic reflexes of freedom and vengeance, the release from bonds that precedes the exercise of willed imperatives.

"Soulfree and Fancyfree"

The suppleness with which Joyce works with the structure of allusion in narrative is such that Stephen's evocation of Monte Cristo's renunciation is of crucial importance to *Portrait* and, later, in a more general, or, as I shall argue [elsewhere], generic sense, to *Ulysses*. But not in the way Stephen initially conceives it. In fact, the Monte Cristo exemplum evaporates at the very moment Stephen hears a story similar to it. As self-romancer, Dedalus experiences a spiritual jolt worse than a whack from Father Dolan's pandy bat when the Jesuit priest at the retreat turns the fable of renunciation inside out. In the hell-fire romance, the priest evokes the plight of the nay-saying rebel angel Lucifer. Refusal becomes a literal disaster—a Miltonic star has his heroic lights put out: "*Non serviam: I will not serve.* That instant was his ruin." Though later in *Portrait* and again in *Ulysses* Dedalus appropriates this exact phrase to abjure the bonds of family, religion, and country, when he first listens to the priest's mimicry of the Satanic utterance it petrifies him. In *Ulysses,* Mulligan still thinks Stephen has been frightened by the Jesuits from any Daedalian or Attic vocation: "—They drove his wits astray, he said, by visions of hell. He will never capture the Attic note."

At the time of the hell-fire sermons, Stephen, to some extent, was already primed for what the Jesuits would do to him. Sex and freedom turned in his mind with a reverse spin from his earlier reveries on Mercedes and Monte Cristo. The postpubescent sexual glut of his evenings in Nighttown had tarnished the cool economy of the Count's refusal. Stephen was a woeful future artificer trapped in Dublin's labyrinth, made queasy by the congealed ingredients of his city and its alphabetical symbols.

> The letters of the name of Dublin lay heavily upon his mind, pushing one another surlily hither and thither with slow boorish insistence. His soul was fattening and con-

gealing into a gross grease, plunging ever deeper in its dull fear into a sombre threatening dusk, while the body that was his stood, listless and dishonoured, gazing out of darkened eyes, helpless, perturbed and human for a bovine god to stare upon.

After the retreat, Stephen travels the only path that remains open to him; he moves toward, rather than from, the communal and communicant fold. He becomes a functionary of religious sodalities; he partakes of the church's sacraments; he eats of the bread and drinks of the wine; and he even considers the priestly role of administering the offering rather than the Cristofian role of abjuring it. But this is an interim consideration. Dedalus's romantic nature resurfaces, and he balks at the ceremonies of a vocation he will soon reject: "To merge his life in the common tide of other lives was harder for him than any fasting or prayer, and it was his constant failure to do this to his own satisfaction which caused in his soul at last a sensation of spiritual dryness together with a growth of doubts and scruples."

The commonness of the action and its attendant obligations turns Stephen away from the priesthood, and his renunciation approaches the substance as well as the rhythm of Monte Cristo's refusal of the muscatel grapes. The text of *Portrait* picks up the beat: "He had refused. Why?" He aims, among other things, to separate himself, to dodge "the challenge of the sentries who had stood as guardians of his boyhood and had sought to keep him among them that he might be subject to them and serve their ends." His refusal to serve extends later to denying his mother's request that he take Easter duty in the church. To partake of the eucharist under a roof that may impose unwanted obligations upon him makes Stephen fear a litmus change in his own nature: "the chemical action which would be set up in my soul by a false homage to a symbol behind which are massed twenty centuries of authority and veneration." Dedalus wants his soul free, as he soon exults, to forge other symbols within its smithy.

The real significance of romantic renunciation, the first hint of which had arrived even before the hell-fire sermons with Stephen's heretical refusal to confess away the sins of a poet like Byron, is its presumed status as the mark of aesthetic integrity. Renunciation may impose the exilic brand of a Byronic Cain, but it also provides an initiatory impetus to action, a prelude to a fabulous career, a self-initiated career that invites freedom in the form of communal abjuration. This is what Dedalus proclaims in *Portrait* and this is what he begins anew the day of *Ulysses,* a good deal of which is spent, with ample drinking but little eating, ridding himself of encumbrances: the Irish Friend (Mulligan), the Irish Job, the Irish Samaritan (Bloom), even the Irish Wife (Molly) who has almost but not quite been offered to him. Stephen himself makes his case in *Ulysses* when theorizing on the beleaguered Shakespeare's manufactured life and vital art: "— There can be no reconciliation, Stephen said, if there has not been a sundering."

The figure who can afford such a renunciatory course must of needs rely on sustaining powers of genius. It is as Albert de Morcerf says of the exile, Monte Cristo, in the romance: " 'I really do look upon him as one of Byron's heroes, whom misery has marked with a fatal brand . . . who, disinherited of their patrimony, have achieved fortune by the force of their adventurous genius, which has placed them above the laws of society' " (*MC*). Fatality is a singling out, a specialness, a dignity, recognized in Monte Cristo and obviously romanticized by Dumas whose hero says to Mercedes: " 'What I most loved after you, Mercedes, was myself, my dignity, and that strength which rendered me superior to other men; that strength was my life.' "

Such superiority knows no bounds, even national ones. Its exilic range is part of its power. As Monte Cristo says to the villainous prosecutor, Villefort, "You believe me to be a Frenchman, for I speak French with the same facility and purity as yourself. Well, Ali, my Nubian, believes me to be an Arab; Bertuccio, my steward, takes me for a Roman; Haydee, my slave, thinks me a Greek." His very range inflates his ego: " 'I am a cosmopolite. No country can say it saw my birth; God alone knows what country will see me die. I adopt all customs, speak all languages. . . . You may therefore comprehend that being of no country, asking no protection from any government, acknowledging no man as my brother, not one of the scruples that arrest the powerful, or the obstacles which paralyse the weak, paralyses or arrests me [*pas un seul des scruples qui arrêtent les puissants ou des obstacles qui paralysent les faibles ne me paralyse ou ne m'arrête*]. I have only two adversaries,—I will not say two conquerors, for with perseverance I subdue even them,—they are time and space.' " It is most likely pure coincidence, but Monte Cristo's vocabulary, *paralyse* and *arrest,* and his vision of supplemental challenge, *time* and *space* (*distance* in the French) seem to have taken independent root in Joyce's own meanderings on aesthetics, whether in relation to the home-grown Irish of *Dubliners* or to the narrative time-space conundrums of *Finnegans Wake.* The real romance that takes place in *Portrait,* the one that will receive its classical form in *Ulysses* and *Finnegans Wake,* is the refabulation of a tale like Dumas's or like Homer's of exile and vengeance into a tale of artistic, cosmopolitan preparedness, a tale substantiated or filled out in Joyce's works that inscribe Ireland as they cast beyond her.

Stephen had inklings in *Portrait* of the direction in which renunciation might point him when, during his first epiphany of an artistic vocation, he saw clouds drifting westward from a Europe that "lay out there beyond the Irish Sea, Europe of strange tongues and valleyed and woodbegirt and citadelled and of entrenched and marshalled races. He heard a confused music within him as of memories and names which he was almost conscious of but could not capture even for an instant." In the same scene, Dedalus looks at his own city and instead of the glut of congealed alphabet imagines all extraterritorial histories and mythologies plunging into Dublin through him. Dublin is pan-European: "A moment before the ghost of the ancient kingdom of the Danes had looked forth through the vesture of the hazewrapped city. Now, at the name of the fabulous artificer, he seemed to hear the noise of dim waves and to see a winged form flying above the waves and slowly climbing the air." The scope extends from Scandinavia to Crete, from the northernmost to the southernmost reaches of Europe, from Odin to Daedalus. Stephen has not yet set pen to paper, but he has moved beyond his native land to the exilic resources of Joyce's later Semitic-Hibernian *Odyssey* and his epic Irish *Wake.*

Dedalus imagines the mysterious Europe and then he sees his vision, the lovely girl on the strand, "his ownest girlie," as Gerty MacDowell might put it. His muse is so stimulated that he seeks a landfall to sleep away his inspiration, still (and perhaps always) libidinous. As he dozes he enters a dream world, a supplement: "His soul was swooning into some new world, fantastic, dim, uncertain as under sea, traversed by cloudy shapes and beings." The opportunity is not unlike that promised by the hashish-peddling Count of Monte Cristo in his island sea cave, though I cite it as a Byronic parallel, not a direct allusion.

"Are you a man of imagination,—a poet? taste this, and the boundaries of possibility disappear; the fields of infinite space open to you; you advance free in heart, free in mind, into the boundless realms of unfettered revelry. Are you ambitious, and do you seek to reach the high places of the earth? taste this, and in an hour you will be a king,—not a king of a petty kingdom hidden in some corner of Europe, like France, Spain, or England, but king of the world, king of the universe, king of creation."

(MC)

To forge a career as king of *his* world or, at least, of its language (*basilicogrammate*), Dedalus prepares himself, as Cranly puts it in *Portrait,* for "the mode of life or of art whereby your spirit could express itself in unfettered freedom." He seeks that exile that neither Odysseus nor Monte Cristo sought, but that found both and made both. Cranly continues: "—Alone, quite alone. You have no fear of that. And you know what that word means? Not only to be separate from all others but to have not even one friend." In *Stephen Hero,* Daedalus had told his brother: "Isolation is the first principle of artistic economy," and now in *Portrait,* Stephen's journal entry for March 21 reads "Free. Soulfree and fancyfree. Let the dead bury the dead. Ay. And let the dead marry the dead." Stephen's exultation upon the totality of release buries the conventionalized libido; his stay-at-home Mercedes, whoever she be, can, like Monte Cristo's, marry none but the barely living dead. Stephen's tactics then acknowledge the exilic program: "I will try to express myself in some mode of life or art as freely as I can and as wholly as I can, using for my defence the only arms I allow myself to use—silence, exile, and cunning."

Joyce's sweet Icarian bird of youth in *Portrait of the Artist* assumes that his aesthetic parabola will fly him by the nets of nationality, language, and religion, though it is one of Joyce's subtle turnarounds as a more mature, substantiating artist to make the innocuous little preposition *by* mean "with" as well as "past." Exile is an impetus, a positioning, and a perspective. As is the case for the general allegory of narrative supplementation I have presented throughout as part of the process of narrative genesis, one gets outside a space to look in and see wholly; on the other hand, the space created from outside is, willy-nilly, a projection, subject to laws generated and inspired by the imagining mind. Stephen's goal is an art whose powers are supreme, whose revenge is complete (satisfied), and whose stance is distant. But his words are initiatory and, as yet, unsubstantiated—they project the fabulous and heroic version of romance and they sound similar to those of the dark avenger, Monte Cristo, who soars like the Daedalian artist: " 'I am free as a bird, and have wings like one. . . . I have my mode of dispensing justice, silent and sure, without respite or appeal, which condemns or pardons, and which no one sees' " (MC).

Chronology

1882 James Augustine Aloysius Joyce born in Dublin on February 2 to John Stanislaus Joyce, tax-collector, and Mary Jane (May) Murray Joyce. He is the eldest of ten children who survive infancy, of whom the closest to him is his next brother Stanislaus (born 1884).

1888–91 Attends Clongowes Wood College, a Jesuit boarding school. He eventually is forced to leave because of his father's financial troubles. During Joyce's childhood and early adulthood, the family moves many times, from respectable suburbs of Dublin to poorer districts, as its size grows and its finances dwindle. Charles Stewart Parnell dies on October 6; the young Joyce writes an elegy, "Et tu, Healy." His father, a staunch Parnellite, has the poem printed, but no copies survive.

1892–98 Briefly attends the less intellectually prestigious Christian Brothers School, then attends Belvedere College, another Jesuit school.

1898–1902 Attends University College (also Jesuit); turns away from Catholicism and Irish nationalist politics. Writes a play, *A Brilliant Career* (which he later destroys), and essays, several of which are published. Graduates in 1902 with a degree in modern languages, having learned French, Italian, German, Norwegian, and Latin. Leaves Dublin to go to Paris and study medicine.

1903 Joyce works primarily on writing poems (which will be published in 1907 as *Chamber Music*) and reading

Jonson at the Bibliothèque Ste. Geneviève. Receives a telegram from his father ("Mother dying come home Father"). Returns to Dublin, where May Joyce dies of cancer on August 13, four months after her son's return.

1904   An essay-narrative, "A Portrait of the Artist," is rejected for publication; several poems are published in various magazines, and a few stories, which eventually appear in *Dubliners,* are published. Stays for a time in the Martello Tower with Oliver St. John Gogarty (Malachi Mulligan in *Ulysses*). Joyce takes his first walk with Nora Barnacle on June 16 ("Bloomsday" in *Ulysses*). The daughter of a Galway baker, she is working in a Dublin boarding house. In October, Joyce and Nora leave for the continent, where they will live the remainder of their lives. Joyce finds work at a Berlitz school in Pola (now in Yugoslavia).

1905   The Joyces (as they are known, although they do not marry until 1931, for "testamentary" reasons) move to Trieste, where Joyce teaches at the Berlitz school. Birth of son Giorgio on July 27. Joyce submits manuscript of *Chamber Music* and *Dubliners* to Dublin publisher Grant Richards. Joyce's brother Stanislaus joins them in Trieste.

1907   After a year in Rome, where Joyce worked in a bank, the Joyces return to Trieste, where Joyce does private tutoring in English. *Chamber Music* published in London (not by Grant Richards). Birth of a daughter, Lucia Anna, on July 26. Writes "The Dead," the last of the stories that will become *Dubliners*. Works on revision of *Stephen Hero,* an adaptation of the essay "A Portrait of the Artist," later to be *A Portrait of the Artist as a Young Man*. Begins writing articles for an Italian newspaper.

1908   Abandons work on *Portrait* after completing three of five projected chapters.

1909   Joyce pays two visits to Dublin: in August, to sign a contract for the publication of *Dubliners* (not with Grant Richards), and in September as representative for a group who wishes to set up the first cinema in Dublin. Returns to Trieste with sister Eva, who will now live with the Joyces.

1910   Cinema venture fails; publication of *Dubliners* delayed.

1911   Publication of *Dubliners* is held up, mainly because of what are feared to be offensive references to Edward VII in "Ivy Day in the Committee Room." Joyce writes to George V to ask if he finds the story objectionable; a secretary replies that His Majesty does not express opinions on such matters.

1912   Final visit to Dublin with his family. Printer destroys the manuscript of *Dubliners,* deciding the book's aims are anti-Irish. Joyce takes the proofs, a set of which he has obtained from his equally unsympathetic publisher, to London but cannot find a publisher for the work there either.

1913   Joyce's original publisher, Grant Richards, asks to see the manuscript of *Dubliners* again. Ezra Pound, at the urging of William Butler Yeats, writes Joyce asking to see some of his work, since Pound has connections with various magazines and might be able to help get Joyce published.

1914   Grant Richards publishes *Dubliners*. At Pound's urging, *A Portrait of the Artist as a Young Man* is published serially by the London magazine *The Egoist.* Joyce begins work on *Ulysses.* World War I begins on August 4.

1915   Joyce completes his play *Exiles.* After Joyce pledges neutrality to the Austrian authorities in Trieste who threatened to intern him, the family moves to Zürich, with the exception of Stanislaus, who is interned. Joyce awarded a British Royal Literary Fund grant, the first of several grants he will receive.

1916   Publishes *A Portrait of the Artist as a Young Man* in book form in New York.

1917   Undergoes the first of numerous eye operations.

1918   Grant Richards publishes *Exiles* in London; it is also published in the United States. The American magazine *The Little Review* begins serializing *Ulysses,* which is not yet complete. Armistice Day, November 11.

1919   Joyce refuses to be analyzed by Carl Jung. *The Egoist* also begins serializing *Ulysses*. The U.S. Post Office confiscates issues of *The Little Review* containing the "Lestrygonians" and the "Scylla and Charybdis" chapters.

1920–21   More issues of *The Little Review* confiscated. In September, John S. Sumner, the secretary of the New York Society for the Prevention of Vice, lodges a protest against the "Nausicaa" issue. The case comes to trial, and the *Review* loses, in February 1921. Publication ceases in the United States. Joyce and family move to Paris. Joyce finishes *Ulysses*. Sylvia Beach agrees to publish it in Paris.

1922   Shakespeare and Company, Sylvia Beach's press, publishes *Ulysses* in Paris on February 2, Joyce's birthday. Nora takes children to Galway for a visit, over Joyce's protests, and their train is fired upon by Irish Civil War combatants.

1923   Joyce begins *Finnegans Wake,* known until its publication as *Work in Progress.*

1924   Part of the *Work* appears in the Paris magazine *transatlantic review.*

1926   Pirated edition of *Ulysses* (incomplete) serialized in New York by *Two Worlds Monthly.*

1927   Shakespeare and Company publishes *Pomes Penyeach.* Parts of *Work* published in Eugene Jolas's *transition,* in Paris.

1928   Joyce publishes parts of *Work* in New York, to protect the copyright.

1929   Joyce assists in a French translation of *Ulysses,* which appears in February. Lucia Joyce's mental stability seems precarious. To his father's delight, Giorgio Joyce makes his debut as a singer, with some success.

1930   At Joyce's instigation, Herbert Gorman begins a biography of Joyce. Joyce supervises a French translation of *Anna Livia Plurabelle,* part of the *Work,* by Samuel Beckett and friends, which appears in the *Nouvelle Revue Française* in 1931. Marriage of son Giorgio to Helen Kastor Fleischman.

1931   Joyce marries Nora Barnacle at a registry office in London. Death of Joyce's father.

1932   Helen Joyce gives birth to a son, Stephen James, on February 15. Joyce writes "Ecce Puer," a poem celebrating the birth of his grandson. Daughter Lucia suffers first mental breakdown; she is diagnosed as hebephrenic (a form of schizophrenia). Bennett Cerf of Random House contracts for the American publication of *Ulysses*.

1933   On December 6, Judge John M. Woolsey admits *Ulysses* into the United States, declaring that "whilst in many places the effect . . . on the reader undoubtedly is somewhat emetic, nowhere does it tend to be an aphrodisiac." Lucia Joyce hospitalized, as she will often be until her permanent hospitalization.

1934   Random House publishes *Ulysses*.

1936   Joyce publishes *Collected Poems* in New York and *A Chaucer A.B.C.* with illuminations by Lucia.

1939   *Finnegans Wake* published in London and New York. War declared. The Joyces move to Vichy, France, to be near Lucia's mental hospital.

1940   Herbert Gorman's authorized biography of Joyce appears. After the fall of France, the Joyces manage once more to get to Zürich.

1941   Joyce dies following surgery on a perforated ulcer on January 13. He is buried in Fluntern Cemetery, in Zürich, with no religious ceremony, at Nora's request.

1951   Nora Barnacle Joyce dies in Zürich on April 10. She is buried in Fluntern as well, but not next to Joyce, since that space has been taken. In 1966, the two bodies are reburied together.

Contributors

HAROLD BLOOM, Sterling Professor of the Humanities at Yale University, is the author of *The Anxiety of Influence, Poetry and Repression,* and many other volumes of literary criticism. His forthcoming study, *Freud: Transference and Authority,* attempts a full-scale reading of all of Freud's major writings. A MacArthur Prize Fellow, he is general editor of five series of literary criticism published by Chelsea House. During 1987–88, he served as Charles Eliot Norton Professor of Poetry at Harvard University.

HUGH KENNER, Professor Emeritus of English at the Johns Hopkins University, is the leading critic of the High Modernists (Pound, Eliot, Joyce) and of Beckett. His books include *The Pound Era, The Stoic Comedians, Dublin's Joyce,* and *Ulysses.* He is currently working on *A Sinking Island,* a book about England.

The late RICHARD ELLMANN, formerly Goldsmiths' Professor of English at New College, Oxford, and Research Professor at Emory University, was perhaps the leading modern literary biographer. He is best known for his books on Joyce and Yeats. Forthcoming is his definitive biography of Oscar Wilde.

ANTHONY BURGESS, author of the Enderby trilogy, *A Clockwork Orange,* and many other novels, has also written critical works, notably on Joyce, Lawrence, Hemingway, and Shakespeare. His most recent work of fiction is *The End of the World News.*

SUZETTE HENKE is Associate Professor of English at the State University of New York at Binghamton. She is the author of *Joyce's Moraculous Sindbook: A Study of* Ulysses and the co-editor, with Elaine Unkeless, of *Women in Joyce.* Her works-in-progress include a book entitled *James Joyce and the Politics of Desire* and a study of autobiographical fiction by contemporary women writers.

MARTIN PRICE is Sterling Professor of English at Yale University. His books include *Swift's Rhetorical Art: A Study in Structure and Meaning, To the Palace of Wisdom: Studies in Order and Energy from Dryden to Blake,* and most recently *Forms of Life: Character and Moral Imagination in the Novel.*

JOHN PAUL RIQUELME teaches in the Department of English at Southern Methodist University. He is the author of *Teller and Tale in Joyce's Fiction: Oscillating Perspectives.*

PATRICK PARRINDER is Reader in English at the University of Reading. His books include *H. G. Wells* (The Critical Heritage Series), *Science Fiction: Its Criticism and Teaching,* and a Cambridge critical study, *James Joyce.*

MICHAEL SEIDEL, Professor of English at Columbia University, is the author of *The Satiric Inheritance: Rabelais and Sterne, Epic Geography,* and *Exile and the Narrative Imagination.*

Bibliography

Adams, Robert M. *James Joyce: Common Sense and Beyond.* New York: Random House, 1967.

Anderson, Chester G. "Baby Tuckoo: Joyce's 'Features of Infancy.' " In *Approaches to Joyce's* Portrait: *Ten Essays,* edited by Thomas F. Staley and Bernard Benstock. Pittsburgh: University of Pittsburgh Press, 1976.

———, ed. A Portrait of the Artist as a Young Man: *Text, Criticism, and Notes.* New York: Viking Press, 1963.

August, Eugene R. "Father Arnall's Use of Scripture in *A Portrait.*" *James Joyce Quarterly* 4 (1967): 275–79.

Beja, Morris, ed. *James Joyce's* Dubliners *and* Portrait: *A Selection of Critical Essays.* London: Macmillan, 1973.

Benstock, Bernard. *James Joyce.* New York: Frederick Ungar, 1985.

———, ed. *The Seventh of Joyce.* Bloomington: Indiana University Press, 1982.

Bidwell, Bruce. *The Joycean Way: A Topographic Guide to* Dubliners *and* A Portrait of the Artist as a Young Man. Dublin: Wolfhound Press, 1981.

Bloom, Harold, ed. *Modern Critical Views: James Joyce.* New Haven: Chelsea House, 1986.

Bowen, Zack. *Musical Allusions in the Works of James Joyce.* Albany: State University of New York Press, 1974.

Bowen, Zack, and James F. Carens, eds. *A Companion to Joyce Studies.* Westport, Conn.: Greenwood, 1984.

Boyd, Elizabeth F. "James Joyce's Hell-Fire Sermons." *MLN* 75 (1960): 561–71.

Boyle, Robert, S.J. *James Joyce's Pauline Vision.* Carbondale: Southern Illinois University Press, 1978.

Brandabur, Edward. *A Scrupulous Meanness.* Urbana: University of Illinois Press, 1971.

Brivic, Sheldon. *Joyce between Freud and Jung.* Port Washington, N.Y.: Kennikat Press, 1980.

———. "Joyce in Progress: A Freudian View." *James Joyce Quarterly* 13 (1976): 306–27.

———. *Joyce the Creator.* Madison: University of Wisconsin Press, 1985.

Brown, Richard. *James Joyce and Sexuality.* Cambridge: Cambridge University Press, 1985.

Burgess, Anthony. *Re Joyce.* New York: Norton, 1965.

————. *Joysprick: An Introduction to the Language of James Joyce*. London: André Deutsch, 1973.

Bushrui, Suheil Badi, and Bernard Benstock, eds. *James Joyce: An International Perspective*. Totowa, N.J.: Barnes & Noble, 1982.

Buttigieg, Joseph A. "Aesthetics and Religion in *A Portrait of the Artist as a Young Man*." *Christianity and Literature* 28, no. 4 (1979): 44–56.

Cervo, Nathan. "'Seeing' as Being: The Blind Apotheosis of Stephen Dedalus." *Northern New England Review* 10 (1983): 52–65.

Chace, William R., ed. *Joyce: A Collection of Critical Essays*. Englewood Cliffs, N.J.: Prentice-Hall, 1974.

Church, Margaret. "*A Portrait* and Giambattista Vico: A Source Study." In *Approaches to Joyce's* Portrait: *Ten Essays,* edited by Thomas F. Staley and Bernard Benstock. Pittsburgh: University of Pittsburgh Press, 1976.

Cixous, Helene. *The Exile of James Joyce*. Translated by Sally A. J. Purcell. New York: David Lewis, 1972.

Collinson, Diane. "The Aesthetic Theory of Stephen Dedalus." *British Journal of Aesthetics* 23, no. 1 (1983): 61–73.

Connolly, Thomas E. "Kinesis and Stasis: Structural Rhythm in Joyce's *Portrait*." *University Review* 3 (1966): 21–30.

Cope, Jackson I. *Joyce's Cities: Archaeologies of the Soul*. Baltimore: Johns Hopkins University Press, 1981.

Cross, Richard K. *Flaubert and Joyce: The Rite of Fiction*. Princeton: Princeton University Press, 1971.

Day, Robert Adams. "How Stephen Wrote His Vampire Poem." *James Joyce Quarterly* 17 (1980): 183–97.

Deming, Robert H. *A Bibliography to James Joyce Studies*. Lawrence: University of Kansas Libraries, 1964.

————, ed. *James Joyce: The Critical Heritage*. 2 vols. New York: Barnes & Noble, 1970.

Dibble, Jerry Allen. "Stephen's Esthetic and Joyce's Art: Theory and Practice of Genre in *A Portrait of the Artist as a Young Man*." *Journal of Narrative Technique* 6 (1976): 29–40.

Doherty, James. "Joyce and *Hell Opened to Christians:* The Edition He Used for His Sermons." *Modern Philology* 61 (1963): 110–19.

Duyfhuizen, Bernard. "'Words [mis]taken': The Opening Sentence of the Retreat Sermons." *James Joyce Quarterly* 16 (1979): 488–90.

Ehrlich, Heyward, ed. *Light Rays: James Joyce and Modernism*. New York: New Horizon, 1984.

Ellmann, Maud. "Dismembering Dedalus." In *Untying the Text: A Post Structuralist Reader,* edited by Robert Young. London: Routledge & Kegan Paul, 1981.

————. "Polytropic Man: Paternity, Identity and Naming in *The Odyssey* and *A Portrait of the Artist as a Young Man*." In *James Joyce: New Perspectives,* edited by Colin MacCabe. Sussex: Harvester Press, 1982. Bloomington: Indiana University Press, 1982.

Ellmann, Richard. *The Consciousness of Joyce*. New York: Oxford University Press, 1977.

————. *James Joyce*. Rev. ed. New York: Oxford University Press, 1982.

Epstein, Edmund L. *The Ordeal of Stephen Dedalus: The Conflict of the Generations in Joyce's* A Portrait of the Artist as a Young Man. Carbondale: Southern Illinois University Press, 1971.

——, ed. *A Starchamber Quiry: A James Joyce Centennial Volume, 1882–1982.* London: Methuen, 1982.

Fleishman, Avrom. *Figures of Autobiography: The Language of Self-Writing in Victorian and Modern England.* Berkeley: University of California Press, 1983.

Fortuna, Diane. "The Labyrinth as Controlling Image in Joyce's *A Portrait of the Artist as a Young Man.*" *Bulletin of the New York Public Library* 76 (1972): 120–80.

Foster, Thomas G. "Joyce's Grammar of Experience." *Eire-Ireland* 17, no. 4 (1982): 19–40.

Frank, Joseph. *The Widening Gyre: Crisis and Mastery in Modern Literature.* Bloomington: Indiana University Press, 1963.

Friedman, Melvin. *Stream of Consciousness: A Study in Literary Method.* New Haven: Yale University Press, 1956.

Garrett, Peter K. *Scene and Symbol from George Eliot to James Joyce: Studies in Changing Fictional Mode.* New Haven: Yale University Press, 1969.

Gifford, Don. *Joyce Annotated: Notes for* Dubliners *and* A Portrait of the Artist as a Young Man. Berkeley: University of California Press, 1982.

Givens, Seon, ed. *James Joyce: Two Decades of Criticism.* New York: Vanguard Press, 1948.

Goldman, Arnold. *The Joyce Paradox: Form and Freedom in His Fiction.* London: Routledge & Kegan Paul, 1966.

Gross, John. *James Joyce.* New York: Viking Press, 1970.

Halper, Nathan. *Studies in Joyce.* Studies in Modern Literature, no. 5. Ann Arbor: UMI Research Press, 1983.

Hayman, David. "Daedalian Imagery in *A Portrait of the Artist as a Young Man.*" In *Hereditas: Seven Essays on the Modern Experience of the Classical,* edited by Frederick Will. Austin: University of Texas Press, 1964.

——. "*A Portrait of the Artist as a Young Man* and *l'Education Sentimentale:* The Structural Affinities." *Orbis Litterarum* 19 (1964): 161–75.

Henke, Suzette, and Elaine Unkeless, eds. *Women in Joyce.* Urbana: University of Illinois Press, 1982.

Herr, Cheryl. *Joyce's Anatomy of Culture.* Urbana: University of Illinois Press, 1986.

Heusel, Barbara Stevens. "The Problems of Figure and Ground in *A Portrait of the Artist as a Young Man.*" *Centennial Review* 26 (1982): 180–98.

Iser, Wolfgang. *The Implied Reader: Patterns of Communication in Prose Fiction from Bunyan to Beckett.* Baltimore: Johns Hopkins University Press, 1974.

James Joyce Quarterly, 1963–.

James Joyce Review, 1957–59.

Kenner, Hugh. *A Colder Eye: The Modern Irish Writers.* New York: Alfred A. Knopf, 1983.

——. "A Cubist Portrait." In *Approaches to Joyce's* Portrait: *Ten Essays,* edited by Thomas F. Staley and Bernard Benstock. Pittsburgh: University of Pittsburgh Press, 1976.

——. *Dublin's Joyce.* London: Chatto & Windus, 1955.

——. *Joyce's Voices.* Berkeley: University of California Press, 1978.

————. *Ulysses*. Rev. ed. Baltimore: Johns Hopkins University Press, 1987.

Kerschner, R. B., Jr. "Time and Language in Joyce's *A Portrait of the Artist as a Young Man*." *ELH* 43 (1976): 604–19.

Kiely, Robert. *Beyond Egotism: The Fiction of James Joyce, Virginia Woolf, and D. H. Lawrence*. Cambridge: Harvard University Press, 1980.

Lawrence, Karen. "Gender and Narrative in *Jacob's Room* and *A Portrait of the Artist as a Young Man*." In *James Joyce: The Centennial Symposium,* edited by Morris Beja, Phillip Herring, Maurice Harmon, and David Norris. Urbana: University of Illinois Press, 1986.

Lemon, Lee T. "*A Portrait of the Artist as a Young Man:* Motif as Motivation and Structure." *Modern Fiction Studies* 12 (1966): 439–50.

Levin, Harry. *James Joyce: A Critical Introduction*. New York: New Directions, 1960.

Litz, A. Walton. *James Joyce*. New York: Twayne, 1966.

Loss, Archie K. *Joyce's Visible Art: The Work of Joyce and the Visual Arts, 1904–1922*. Studies in Modern Literature, no. 38. Ann Arbor: UMI Research Press, 1984.

MacCabe, Colin. *James Joyce and the Revolution of the Word*. London: Macmillan, 1978.

————, ed. *James Joyce: New Perspectives*. Bloomington: Indiana University Press, 1982.

Magalaner, Marvin. *Time of Apprenticeship: The Fiction of Young James Joyce*. New York: Abelard-Schuman, 1959.

Magalaner, Marvin, and Richard M. Kain. *Joyce: The Man, the Work, the Reputation*. Westport, Conn.: Greenwood, 1979.

McCormack, W. J., and Alistair Stead, eds. *James Joyce and Modern Literature*. London: Routledge & Kegan Paul, 1982.

McKnight, Jeanne. "Unlocking the Word-Hoard: Madness, Identity and Creativity in James Joyce." *James Joyce Quarterly* 14 (1972): 420–33.

Modern Fiction Studies 15 (1969). Special James Joyce issue.

Moseley, Virginia. *Joyce and the Bible*. DeKalb: Northern Illinois University Press, 1967.

Murillo, L. A. *The Cyclical Night: Irony in James Joyce and Jorge Luis Borges*. Cambridge: Harvard University Press, 1968.

Naremore, James. "Consciousness and Society in *A Portrait of the Artist*." In *Approaches to Joyce's* Portrait: *Ten Essays,* edited by Thomas F. Staley and Bernard Benstock. Pittsburgh: University of Pittsburgh Press, 1976.

Oates, Joyce Carol. "Jocoserious Joyce." *Critical Inquiry* 2 (1976): 677–88.

Paliwal, B. "The Artist as Creator in *A Portrait of the Artist as a Young Man*." *Literary Criterion* 10 (1971): 44–49.

Parrinder, Patrick. *James Joyce*. Cambridge: Cambridge University Press, 1984.

Peake, C. H. *James Joyce: The Citizen and the Artist*. Stanford: Stanford University Press, 1977.

Peterson, Richard F., Alan M. Cohn, and Edmund L. Epstein, eds. *Work in Progress: Joyce Centenary Essays*. Carbondale: Southern Illinois University Press, 1983.

Reddick, Bryan. "The Importance of Tone in the Structural Rhythm of Joyce's *Portrait*." *James Joyce Quarterly* 6 (1969): 201–17.

Redford, Grant A. "The Role of Structure in Joyce's *Portrait*." *Modern Fiction Studies* 4 (1958): 21–30.

Reid, B. L. "Gnomon and Order in Joyce's *Portrait*." *Sewanee Review* 92 (1984): 397–420.

Reynolds, Mary T. *Joyce and Dante: The Shaping Imagination*. Princeton: Princeton University Press, 1981.

Ricardou, Jean. "Time of the Narration, Time of the Fiction." Translated by Joseph Kestner. *James Joyce Quarterly* 16 (1978/1979): 7–15.

Rice, Thomas Jackson. *James Joyce: A Guide to Research*. New York: Garland, 1983.

Robinson, K. E. "The Stream of Consciousness Technique and the Structure of Joyce's *Portrait*." *James Joyce Quarterly* 9 (1971): 63–84.

Rossman, Charles. "Stephen Dedalus and the Spiritual-Heroic Refrigerating Apparatus: Art and Life in Joyce's *Portrait*." In *Forms of Modern British Fiction*, edited by Alan Warren Friedman. Austin: University of Texas Press, 1975.

Ryan, John, ed. *A Bash in the Tunnel: James Joyce by the Irish*. London: Clifton Books, 1970.

Schlossman, Beryle. *Joyce's Catholic Comedy of Language*. Madison: University of Wisconsin Press, 1985.

Scholes, Robert. "Joyce and the Epiphany: The Key to the Labyrinth?" *Sewanee Review* 72 (1964): 65–77.

———. "Stephen Dedalus: *Eiron* and *Alazon*." *Texas Studies in Literature and Language* 3 (1961): 8–15.

———. "Stephen Dedalus: Poet or Aesthete?" *PMLA* 79 (1964): 484–89.

Scholes, Robert, and Richard M. Kain, eds. *The Workshop of Daedalus: James Joyce and the Raw Materials for* A Portrait of the Artist as a Young Man. Evanston, Ill.: Northwestern University Press, 1965.

Schutte, William M., ed. *Twentieth-Century Interpretations of* A Portrait of the Artist as a Young Man. Englewood Cliffs, N.J.: Prentice-Hall, 1968.

Scott, Bonnie Kime. *Joyce and Feminism*. Bloomington: Indiana University Press, 1984. Sussex: Harvester Press, 1984.

Senn, Fritz. *Joyce's Dislocations: Essays on Reading as Translation*. Edited by John Paul Riquelme. Baltimore: Johns Hopkins University Press, 1984.

Smith, John B. *Imagery and the Mind of Stephen Dedalus: A Computer-Assisted Study of Joyce's* A Portrait of the Artist as a Young Man. Lewisburg, Penn.: Bucknell University Press, 1980.

Staley, Thomas F., and Bernard Benstock, eds. *Approaches to Joyce's* Portrait: *Ten Essays*. Pittsburgh: University of Pittsburgh Press, 1976.

Sucksmith, Harvey Peter. *James Joyce:* A Portrait of the Artist as a Young Man. London: Edward Arnold, 1973.

Sullivan, Kevin. *Joyce among the Jesuits*. New York: Columbia University Press, 1957.

Thrane, James R. "Joyce's Sermon on Hell: Its Sources and Backgrounds." *Modern Philology* 57 (1960): 172–98.

Tindall, William York. *James Joyce: His Way of Interpreting the Modern World*. New York: Charles Scribner's Sons, 1950.

———. "Joyce's Chambermade Music." *Poetry* 80 (1952): 105–16.

———. *The Literary Symbol*. Bloomington: Indiana University Press, 1974.

———. *A Reader's Guide to James Joyce*. New York: Noonday, 1965.

Tucker, Lindsey. *Stephen and Bloom at Life's Feast: Alimentary Symbolism and the Creative Process in James Joyce's* Ulysses. Columbus: Ohio State University Press, 1984.

Weinstein, Philip M. *The Semantics of Desire: Changing Models of Identity from Dickens to Joyce*. Princeton: Princeton University Press, 1984.

Wilds, Nancy G. "Style and Auctorial Presence in *A Portrait of the Artist as a Young Man*." *Style* 7 (1973): 39–55.

Zingrone, Frank. "Joyce and D'Annunzio: The Marriage of Fire and Water." *James Joyce Quarterly* 16 (1979): 253–65.

Acknowledgments

"The *Portrait* in Perspective" by Hugh Kenner from *Dublin's Joyce* by Hugh Kenner, © 1956 by Hugh Kenner. Reprinted by permission of Indiana University Press.

"A Portrait of the Artist as Friend" by Richard Ellmann from *The Kenyon Review* 18, no. 1 (Winter 1956), © 1956 by Kenyon College. Reprinted by permission.

"Martyr and Maze-maker" by Anthony Burgess from *Re Joyce* by Anthony Burgess, © 1965 by Anthony Burgess. Reprinted by permission of W. W. Norton & Co. and Faber & Faber Ltd.

"Stephen Dedalus and Women: A Portrait of the Artist as a Young Misogynist" by Suzette Henke from *Women and Joyce* edited by Suzette Henke and Elaine Unkeless, © 1982 by the Board of Trustees of the University of Illinois. Reprinted by permission.

"The Beauty of Mortal Conditions: Joyce's *A Portrait of the Artist*" (originally entitled "The Beauty of Mortal Conditions: Joyce, Woolf, Mann") by Martin Price from *Forms of Life* by Martin Price, © 1983 by Yale University. Reprinted by permission of Yale University Press.

"The Preposterous Shape of Portraiture: *A Portrait of the Artist as a Young Man*" by John Paul Riquelme from *Teller and Tale in Joyce's Fiction: Oscillating Perspectives* by John Paul Riquelme, © 1983 by the Johns Hopkins University Press, Baltimore/London. Reprinted by permission.

"Joyce's *Portrait* and the Proof of the Oracle" (originally entitled "*A Portrait of the Artist* and *Exiles*") by Patrick Parrinder from *James Joyce* by Patrick Parrinder, © 1984 by Cambridge University Press. Reprinted with permission.

"Monte Cristo's Revenge and Joyce's *A Portrait of the Artist*" (originally entitled "Monte Cristo's Revenge: Joyce's *A Portrait of the Artist* and *Ulysses*") by Michael Seidel from *Exile and the Narrative Imagination* by Michael Seidel, © 1986 by Yale University. Reprinted by permission of Yale University Press.

Index